Emotional and Behavioural Difficulties

Roy Howarth and Pam Fisher

continuum
LONDON • NEW YORK

Continuum International Publishing Group

The Tower Building
11 York Road
London
SE1 7NX

15 East 26th Street
New York, NY 10010

www.continuumbooks.com

British Library Cataloguing-in-Publication Data
A catalogue record for this book is available from the British Library.

ISBN: 08264 7580 9 (paperback)

Typeset by Servis Filmsetting Ltd, Manchester
Printed and bound in Great Britain by MPG Books Ltd, Bodmin,
Cornwall

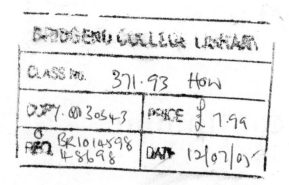

Contents

Introduction

For all involved in teaching, from students to mature members of the profession, pupils with Emotional and Behavioural Difficulties (EBD) are ever present.

They bump into the boundaries of class and school so often they have a good map of right and wrong, can do, must not do. What is difficult to understand is why they spend most of their school life making the wrong choices. Banging their heads against a wall seems to give no pain. They nearly always try to use the toilets or that area round the corner where no one can see, especially from the staffroom, as their headquarters and smoking area. They go the wrong way down corridors, ascend stairs in forbidden ways, need to go to the toilet all the time and forget homework, PE kit, pens and books. They always have problems with school uniform, report books, detentions, lunchtimes and school assemblies. They are lonely or get into fights. They choose the wrong mates. They can be rude and unrewarding.

These difficulties they have in perceiving and accepting boundaries and understanding social relationships and interactions are their Special Educational Needs. Choosing to accept and understand this fact rather than perceiving them as just getting in the way of your teaching is a much more empathetic and enlightened way of working.

The strategies described in this book have been developed and honed during our working life in an EBD special school where, over twenty-five years, pupils have presented us with the whole array of dysfunctional behaviour. Through outreach, managing pupils on phased reintegration programmes and in-service training in mainstream schools and universities, we have exported the expertise gained.

This book aims to support you in your efforts to successfully manage these pupils by helping you to develop a repertoire of effective strategies, tactics and skills. The path we describe is not an easy one but it is very exciting, stimulating and, like the pupils, challenging.

Integrate some of our techniques into your work and we hope you will be agreeably surprised by the results.

1

Defining EBD

We suspect all teachers in mainstream schools find the pupils who have been identified with the Special Educational Need of Emotional and Behavioural Difficulties challenging and frustrating to teach. You are well within your rights to imagine the letters to stand for

Extremely Bloody Difficult
Every Bloody Day

as this is how these pupils can often present in class.

Rather dauntingly we find ourselves, at the very beginning of a book on EBD, struggling to give a clear classification. We are in good company. Specialists have struggled to write a clear definition for those children who are troublesome both in school and in society. Keep in mind that this is not a new problem. These pupils have always been around and many have been challenged before you!

In 1955 the Underwood Report (the first report on *Maladjusted Children* commissioned by a British government) described a maladjusted child as 'one who is disturbed by or disturbs a normal situation'.

The document *Pupils with Problems* (Circular 9/94) describes them as follows:

their problems are clearer and greater than sporadic naughtiness or moodiness and yet not so great as to be classed as mental illness . . . EBD may show through withdrawn, depressive, aggressive or self-injurious tendencies. There may be one or many causes. Family environments or physical or sensory impairments may be associated. (DFE, 1994: 4)

Pupils with EBD, as defined in the circular, always have Special Educational Needs.

Whether the pupil is judged to have EBD will depend on the nature, frequency, persistence, severity, abnormality or cumulative effect of the behaviour compared with normal expectations for a child of the age concerned. There is no absolute definition. (p. 4)

Pupils displaying Emotional and Behavioural Difficulties undoubtedly take up a great deal of time and energy in schools. They are often the most prevalent, least liked and least understood of all pupils with SEN.

Whether they 'act out', i.e. demonstrate aggressive, threatening, disruptive and attention-seeking behaviour openly, or 'act in', i.e. appear anxious, depressed, withdrawn, passive or unmotivated, they all have barriers to learning which, as with any pupil with SEN, will need to be addressed (Scottish Executive, 2004).

Making a conscious shift in your thinking about these pupils from labelling them bad, mad or sad, to understanding that they have Special Educational Needs will help you to be more positive and objective in your management. Although there is no absolute definition of EBD there is general agreement among knowledgeable professionals that pupils with this SEN will tend to fulfil more than one of the following criteria:

- they will be boys rather than girls. Our EBD special school (Years 1–8) had 5 girls on a roll of 78 children. As many as 82 per cent of pupils excluded from mainstream schools in 2002/03 were boys

- have parents or carers who are unable to exercise appropriate controls and could have experienced similar problems as a child.

- one or both carers suffering poor mental health.

- in Local Authority care

- come from lower social groupings where poverty is an issue

- have been physically and/or sexually abused, or witnessed violence and abuse

- have poor social skills and fewer friends

- receive less praise for their work and have fewer positive child/adult interactions

- have low academic self-image

- underachieve or have general/specific learning difficulties

- have poor child/adult skills

- find criticism hard to accept

- be emotionally volatile

- have problems with self-esteem, both high and low.

Self-esteem

In recent times low self-esteem has been one of the most popular and frequently invoked psychological explanations for children's behavioural and social problems. In 2001 Professor Nicholas Emler undertook a review of available research evidence on the effects or causes of low self-esteem (Emler, 2001). Surprisingly one of his key findings was that young people who hold racist attitudes, reject social pressures from adults and peers, and engage in physically risky pursuits such as drink driving or driving too fast have very high self-esteem.

Physical and sexual abuse were identified as especially damaging for children's feelings of self-worth.

The most important influences on young people's level of self-esteem were found to be their parents.

It would therefore be inadvisable to assume that EBD is always an expression of low self-esteem.

The causes of EBD

What causes these young people to develop this complex, pervasive and challenging disability?

We can identify three main areas of causation.

1. Heredity

Pupils may have inherited a genetic predisposition to a specific disorder. These could include Attention Deficit Disorder (ADD), Attention Deficit Hyperactivity Disorder (ADHD), Tourette's syndrome, personality disorders, the autistic spectrum, learning difficulties, sensory impairments, dyspraxia, and language and communication disorders. These may impact on a pupil's ability to happily access the mainstream curriculum with their peers, resulting in a display of challenging and difficult behaviour.

2. Family and society

In their extensive study of psychosocial disorders in young people, Michael Rutter and Donald Smith found that since the early 1950s, with better living conditions, physical health has improved (Rutter and Smith, 1995). However, against expectations, psychosocial disorders have become substantially more prevalent:

♦ crime shows a strong upward trend

♦ alcohol and drug abuse show a massive increase

♦ there has been a rise in depressive conditions in the most recent birth cohorts

♦ suicide and suicidal behaviours are on the increase, especially in boys.

The reasons for these trends include:

♦ increase in family discord and break up. The number of divorces has increased over six times since 1961 and there has been a significant rise in single parenting (at the special school where we worked, an average of 75 per cent of the pupils did not live with both natural parents)

♦ lengthening of the adolescent period due to the falling age of puberty and the rising age of finishing education, which has led to the growth of a strong youth culture

♦ young people being influenced in their behaviour by what they see and hear on the media

♦ increasing affluence and an associated growth in people's expectations that can be difficult to fulfil, resulting in disaffection and anger.

As far as moral values within society are concerned, today's young people are:

♦ more tolerant

♦ less respectful of traditional values

♦ more demanding of autonomy and control

♦ more tolerant of self-interest, minor illegality and personal sexual morality

♦ less confident of major institutions

♦ increasingly emphasizing self-realization and fulfilment.

3. Schools

In the Department for Education circular *Education for Disaffected Pupils* (DFE, 1990–92) the following common strands were found in schools where standards of behaviour were unsatisfactory:

♦ verbal and physical aggression were extensive

♦ physical aggression verging on assault occurred in circulation areas

- reports of intimidation, extortion and bullying were rife

- many lessons were disrupted by unruly pupils

- staff had few skills to defuse difficult situations

- on occasions staff fuelled difficult situations by taking inappropriate confrontational stances

- staff made threats they couldn't carry out

- standards of achievement were unsatisfactory.

It is therefore important to understand that schools themselves, through poor management systems, can increase the incidence of EBD.

Assessment

Given the high incidence of pupils with varying degrees of this SEN in mainstream school, you would expect an effective assessment tool to be available. We began searching for such a tool in the early 1970s.

In the busy environment of school the available tools such as the Rutter scale for teachers and the Bristol Social Adjustment Guides, as used in the National Child Development Study, lacked the simplicity for which we were searching.

In 1988 we modified an assessment tool used in the Inner London Education Authority (ILEA) Junior School Project (Mortimore, 1987). We have used it ever since (see Figure 1.1). This tool, which scores pupils in three areas of development – Emotional, Social and Learning – three times a year, has proved, over time, to be a reliable diagnostic indicator of the severity of the pupil's

Emotional and Behavioural Difficulties

Behaviour Assessment							
Name _____ class _____ date ___ / ___ / ___							
EMOTIONAL	1	2	3	4	5		scores
Happy and contented						Unhappy and anxious	
Copes easily with new situations/people						Difficult with new situations/people	
Even tempered and easy going						Irritable or quarrelsome	
Positive self-image						Negative self-image	
total							
LEARNING	1	2	3	4	5		scores
Concentrates well, not easily distracted						Cannot concentrate on task, distractible	
Eager to learn, curious and contented						Shows little curiosity, no work motivation	
Perseveres if work is difficult/challenging						Lacks perseverance with work	
Can work independently						Needs constant help and encouragement	
total							
CONDUCT	1	2	3	4	5		scores
Helpful, considerate towards others						Bullies or is spiteful towards others	
Sociable and friendly						Solitary and withdrawn	
Readily accepts discipline and control						Generally disruptive or disobedient	
Can ignore difficult behaviour						Joins in disruption	
total							
COMMENTS?							

Fig. 1.1. Behaviour assessment tool

EBD and his/her subsequent progress. It has proved useful as a predictor of the child's ability to cope with the difficult process of reintegrating from a special school to a mainstream setting and has clearly indicated when children were experiencing significant stress as a result of changing foster homes, being reintroduced to a natural parent, or starting a new treatment regime such as drugs or play therapy.

We have also used this tool effectively in mainstream school to assess levels of difficulty in both class groups and individual pupils.

Treatment

The need for multi-agency work in meeting the often complex range of needs of pupils with EBD is well recognized (Cole *et al.*, 1998).

Pupils with EBD often exhibit a confusion of symptoms which can encompass home, community, the medical profession, the police, social services and education. For example, the medical profession may be treating the pupil for a specific disorder. Ritalin, as a treatment for ADD and ADHD, continues to be very much in vogue. For some pupils it undoubtedly helps them to be more effective learners. However, as the symptoms of ADD and ADHD often mirror those of abuse, deprivation and attachment disorders, this is an area which requires constant monitoring.

Social services may be working with the family, giving support and direction. The pupil may be in the care of the Local Authority. The pupil could be offending so the police may be involved. A psychologist may have the pupil on a special programme.

However, of all the professional agencies, it is school that more often than not carries the day-to-day responsibility for helping these pupils. School is where they spend a considerable proportion of their time and are legally meant to be. For schools, difficulties in bringing together the wide number of professional bodies involved in working with a particular EBD pupil and agreeing a uniform approach for treatment can be extremely daunting, frustrating, time consuming and at times almost impossible.

Schools often find that support from other agencies is not of the quality required by these very disturbed pupils.

Summary

There is no precise definition of what constitutes Emotional and Behavioural Difficulties, and the tools available to us for their assessment and treatment are confusing or difficult to co-ordinate.

As these pupils are very often unlikable and 'in your face', threatening your competence and significantly disturbing the calm atmosphere of your classroom, it is very hard for teachers not to label them as naughty or bad.

The majority of these pupils are, in reality, very unhappy, hovering as they do on the fringes of society. They are disabled from functioning normally by a complex interaction of causes ranging from genetic factors, through family difficulties including being exposed to physical and/or sexual abuse, to the pressures of a changing society. They are emotionally volatile and lack those qualities of stability and robustness which enable other pupils to survive similar pressures intact.

This could seem a very bleak picture indeed; however, as this book will explain, there is a great deal we can do in schools to help these pupils to become better adjusted and happier individuals. Schools and you as a teacher may not be able to change their whole world, but you can be a great therapeutic force in their lives.

2

You as a Teacher

You have chosen this exciting and challenging profession. You remember from your own school days the huge variations in teachers' characters, dress, confidence, charisma, voices and teaching styles. During your time in school you clearly identified your favourite teachers and knew what made them special.

It is no different today. You bring to your work a unique appearance, style and personality which pupils identify as you. Of course, it is important to know and celebrate the qualities which make you unique. However, just as we ask pupils to sometimes change their behaviour, you must also be prepared to look honestly and critically at your teacher self.

Your average pupil understands social interaction, will be tolerant of your minor idiosyncrasies and will modify his/her responses accordingly. Pupils with EBD lack this social ability and are hypersensitive to perceived slights.

You can be irritable during a lesson and average Susan will raise her eyebrows and keep a low profile. EBD Charlotte will believe your irritation is personally directed at her and will quickly start creating difficulties.

It is important to be self-critical. Teachers who grow in stature have a degree of humility, build on their strengths and learn from their mistakes.

Your personality

It is well known that pupils value teachers who listen to and respect them, who have a sense of humour, and who can control the class.

Does your personality enable you to demonstrate these qualities, or do you need to modify your natural self? Perhaps you'd benefit from being:

♦ louder/quieter

♦ more assertive/less assertive

♦ calmer/more dynamic

♦ funnier/more serious

♦ less/more friendly

♦ taller in stance

♦ more confident in your appearance?

You might not be perfect and perhaps need a tweak or two.

Your ability to manage personal stress

All teachers at times feel angry, depressed, frustrated and guilty when dealing with difficult students and difficult classes. Upsetting feelings are not only to be expected but are essential and beneficial. They signal the need for change and problem solving, and provide motivation. Danger arises, however, when these feelings so over-whelm teachers that they're immobilized by depression or lose control of their anger. (Webster-Stratton, 1999: 1)

In addition to experiencing emotions of the kind identified here, another reaction is to become shell shocked and give in, giggling madly and joking about who cares anyway.

Without question, at some point in your teaching week you will be confronted by difficult and challenging behaviour. The insight you have into the way you respond to stress will determine how buoyant you feel about your work.

If a group in your class is being difficult what do you think?

(a) 'This class is impossible to teach and I don't like them at all' – you become angry and start criticizing the pupils and shouting at them.

(b) 'It's all my fault for being a poor teacher. There's nothing I can do' – you feel tentative and depressed and avoid disciplining the pupils.

(c) 'I'm going to have to remind these pupils of my classroom expectations' – you focus your thoughts on your ability to cope and be calm.

(d) 'I'm going to try a new strategy and see what happens' – you learn from your actions and develop effective practices.

It is important to be aware of your thoughts and whether you are fundamentally a positive or a negative thinker. Too much negative thinking when faced with a challenging pupil or group will tend to exacerbate the stress you and they are feeling, so aim to increase your positive thoughts and keep calm.

Your interpersonal skills with pupils

Managing a complex and disparate group of individuals is a challenging task requiring considerable skills. You need to be able to pick up a myriad of subtle social signals relating to sub-groups, cliques and individual pupils. Are you able to use this information to help you to socially engineer the class, or is this a skill you need to develop?

Your interpersonal skills with colleagues

Schools contain a hugely varied group of adults performing a great number of complex tasks. The more staff who are loyal and supportive members of the team, bringing to it their positive qualities and support, the happier and more effective the school is going to be.

Your verbal communication skills

Verbal communication is one of your primary tools. Your natural voice may be very quiet or you might, by nature, be a 'wind bag'. However, if you are able to speak with a clear and pleasant voice, varying tone, volume and pace, make your instructions precise and clear, give interesting, stimulating and carefully paced presentations, and aim to use positive language as much as you can, you and your class will benefit.

Your writing skills

Your natural handwriting may be scrawly, untidy, too small or too large. Translating this onto a whiteboard or an interactive board will not help your pupils, particularly those with EBD who often lack academic self-confidence and easily panic if confronted with information that is difficult to read.

Try hard to ensure that your whiteboard writing is clear, well laid out, attractive and precise. Practise this skill. It really makes a difference. When writing in pupils' books is your writing legible and to the point?

Your dress sense

Many schools have opted for a clearly prescribed uniform for all pupils. This uniform can be very strict and rigorously enforced. It may not be your natural style, but in such a climate it is important that teachers also dress smartly. This doesn't imply stuffiness. Pupils appreciate teachers with style. However, there should be an agreement among staff about what constitutes a well-dressed teacher. For example, candy-striped leggings and a tank top may not be deemed to be appropriate.

The longest and most aggressive staff meeting we ever experienced was related to the wearing of leggings and denim by members of staff.

Well-dressed teachers signal to pupils, parents and visiting professionals that they merit respect.

Smelling good also helps. Mothballs, cigarette smoke, or last night's garlic and fried onions are not appropriate. A quick deodorizing spray and mouth wash can work wonders.

Your administrative abilities

Today's teachers are expected to fulfil a vast array of administrative duties. Requests for detailed curriculum planning, reports, incident recording, marking, letters home, performance management data, Individual Education Plans (IEPs), etc. constantly pile up on your desk. If you are by nature a spontaneous, disorganized person and apply this quality to your admin, you are heading for trouble. You will always be playing catch up and this will add to your stress levels. It is essential to have a clear understanding of priorities. Some tasks won't wait while others, if you leave them, will vanish unnoticed from the bottom of the pile. If you find it hard to see the wood from the trees ask for help with management and learn to prioritize.

Summary

Summarize your dominant personality traits. Look at the words/phrases in the box below. Tick the characteristics which apply to you and consider their implications for your classroom performance.

Emotional and Behavioural Difficulties

Your personality? Tick how you think you are
quiet   noisy   shy   confident   good sense of humour sensitive   attractive   calm   irritable   prone to panic   lively inconsistent   positive   disaffected   enthusiastic   supportive understanding   consistent   fair   positively assertive   boring unconfident   clear   negative   tentative   decisive

Key attributes

Rate yourself on the charts below with 5 denoting excellent skills.

Your ability to manage personal stress	1	2	3	4	5
1. Are you able to decrease your negative thoughts?					
2. Do you strive for a positive mindset?					
3. Are you objective when things are difficult?					
4. Can you remain calm in a crisis?					

Your interpersonal skills with pupils	1	2	3	4	5
1. How good are you at sensing inter-pupil dynamics?					
2. How sensitive are you to pupils with social difficulties?					
3. How empathetic are you towards pupils with emotional problems?					
4. Do pupils identify positively with you?					

Your interpersonal skills with colleagues	1	2	3	4	5
1. Do you offer your colleagues support?					
2. Do you ask more experienced staff for help if you need it?					
3. Are you loyal to the Head and Senior Staff Team?					
4. Do you share effective strategies with your colleagues?					

Your verbal communication skills	1	2	3	4	5
1. Do you use your volume level as an effective tool for class management?					
2. Are your verbal presentations clear and interesting?					
3. Do you use low-key, quiet talking to challenging pupils?					
4. Do you use a ratio of praise to negative comments of 4 to 1?					

Your writing skills	1	2	3	4	5
1. Is your writing clear and legible to all the class?					
2. Is it easy to understand work written on the board?					
3. Do you use word-processing for work-sheets and are they smart and attractive?					
4. Do you write clearly and legibly in pupils' books?					

Emotional and Behavioural Difficulties

Your dress sense	1	2	3	4	5
1. Do you believe it is important, as a teacher, to dress well?					
2. Do you smell pleasant?					
3. Do your clothes express your personality appropriately?					
4. Do you follow the staff dress code?					

Your administrative abilities	1	2	3	4	5
1. Are you able to prioritize?					
2. Do you meet deadlines?					
3. Do you use computers to ease your admin load?					
4. Is your desk/office well organized?					

Rating	0–5	6–10	11–15	16–20
Your ability to manage personal stress				
Your interpersonal skills with pupils				
Your interpersonal skills with colleagues				
Your verbal communication skills				
Your writing skills				
Your dress sense				
Your administrative abilities				

If you score yourself under 10 in a section, think about how you can get advice and support to improve your effectiveness in this area. There are many kind and highly skilled people in schools who will be delighted to help you.

EBD pupils, more than any others, are likely to raise your levels of stress by questioning your competence as a teacher. You will be much more likely to work successfully with these challenging pupils if you objectively examine your abilities and make appropriate adjustments to your professional behaviour.

3

Your Teaching Room

The room where you teach is your domain; it is your territory, your kingdom, home for the day and your place of work. You state what happens, when and in what order. That is your responsibility as a teacher.

For many EBD pupils territory is hugely important. The domination of space – a room, a toilet, a corridor and especially your classroom – is a target. Although the disruptive pupil often has a low *academic* self-image, his/her *actual* self-image can be high and demanding ('Jack the Lad'; leader of the sub-culture). Indeed, if you have a low academic self-image, the control of the teaching room is essential if you are to maintain your high self-image.

Pupils will find many ways of questioning who manages the territory. The teaching room is therefore the place where, to put it mildly, you are going to clash. How you set up your room and how you present it as a place of work signals to your pupils what you expect and defines your attitude to management, learning and teaching. As pupils walk into your room they will look for signposts as to what is allowed and what is not, what they can get away with, what is forbidden and what is celebrated. EBD pupils are like water flowing into a newly made pond. They will look for the cracks, the mistakes, the design flaws. Is it level? Is it fair? Does it work as it should do?

The whole point about teaching-room design is to state clearly what is going to happen, the kind of teacher you are and how enjoyable learning is. Good rooms radiate the feeling, as you walk in, that expectations of behaviour are high and that they are about learning and improving.

The geography of your teaching room

How you arrange your teaching room can have a very significant effect on behaviour and learning.

EBD pupils can spot weaknesses in layout very quickly and use the errors to their negative advantage. The parts of the room just out of the teacher's sight, for example next to switches, near the door, right at the back and out of reach, beside a window that opens, near the computer, sitting with 'mates', are magnets for these pupils. Removing the majority of pitfalls can change the whole atmosphere.

The main components of the room are:

- ♦ shape and size
- ♦ doors and windows
- ♦ seating
- ♦ mobility
- ♦ wall space
- ♦ furniture
- ♦ equipment.

Shape and size

The shape and size of your teaching room is more often than not presented to you as a *fait accompli*. Unfortunately it has not always been designed with teaching as its main focus. Rooms can be long, L-shaped, too big or too small; some have more than one door and are full of windows, while others have too few windows or windows that face the playground!

If the room is too big make sure your teaching base (either your desk or where you stand) is close to the main trouble-makers, as too far away can mean delays in giving attention. Distance also allows difficult pupils the time and space to create little territories which, within minutes, form into empires.

Doors and windows

Doors should be taken into consideration when designing the seating arrangements. Some pupils love to control who comes in and who goes out. Doors provide a way out to the toilet or an escape route for those wanting a crafty smoke 'round the back' of school (and for lots of other nasty activities besides that), so make sure that pupils with EBD are not near the gateway and that you're in control of it.

Try to face the class away from windows so that activities outside or roaming pupils don't interfere with your lessons. Window blinds or curtains are not difficult to put up and can help a great deal. They can reduce sunlight, cool the room down and negate outside stimuli. We have been in rooms where the blinds are drawn all day. I would not recommend this (pupils could go stir crazy), the selective use of blinds or curtains can be very helpful.

Seating

Arrange the seating in a way that allows you to see everyone's face and make sure they can see you without having to be yoga experts. Ensure that there are no corners for hiding in.

Do your teaching from where you can see everyone. In the case of the L-shaped room, standing in the corner will enable you to see both parts of the room. Remember, EBD pupils know the hidden corners.

As crowding tends to raise noise levels and increase tension, seating arrangements in a small room are crucial to the smooth running of the class. Try to:

♦ surround a difficult pupil with stable ones

♦ be strict about where pupils sit

♦ think about how pupils are seated, e.g. boy/girl, tables of boys and tables of girls, in alphabetical order, seating that keeps cliques and sub-groups separate

♦ consider changing the seating each week to reward good behaviour.

Think about changing seating for different types of lesson, for example group lessons, individual study time, screen watching, whiteboard instruction and so on. You should always keep control of who sits where and for how long. This arrangement does not have to be oppressive; however, it is one of the keys to creating the correct environment for teaching. If you are managing a particularly difficult EBD pupil, his/her seating arrangement should be written in the IEP (see Chapter 6).

Mobility

There is a close link between seating and mobility. Movement in and out of and around the teaching room (out of seat) is prime time for pupils with EBD to wreak havoc. Controlling movement into, out of and around the classroom is a sensible way of reducing a clutch of behaviours. Who moves when and where should be the responsibility of the teacher alone.

> We have observed classes where, by the middle of the lesson, more than 40 per cent of the pupils were on the move, and 50 per cent of the movement was not work related. This was not an environment suited for 'learning'.

Entering the room is the start of your interaction with the class and therefore sets the tone for your lesson. We strongly advise that you greet your pupils at the door before they are allowed to enter then manage their admission to your domain in a way that you feel is appropriate. It is a good time to be positive and cheerful with your EBD pupils. Make them feel good and special on your first contact. Don't ignore them or turn your back on them.

Once all the pupils are settled in the room you must be able to gain silence before the lesson can start. There are many ways to achieve this:

♦ stand with your arms folded, scanning the room

♦ quietly, repeatedly ask for silence

♦ raise your hand and ask all silent members of the class to do the same

♦ ask everyone initially to stand and then seat them when they are silent.

If silence is not achieved then ask everyone to stand and do not reseat pupils until everyone is silent.

Your EBD pupils will find initial silence difficult. Support them by praising their compliance. If you start a lesson in confusion, with some pupils not listening to your introduction or initial instructions, the class will not see you as the leader of the group.

Describe how pupils are to move around the room and when. One-way systems around the classroom can help a lot. Make sure the pathways are as wide and obstacle free as possible.

In the case of art rooms, gyms, labs, etc., many of which can't be physically changed, the procedures for mobility are crucial. When a space is to be entered, who can move from one part of the room to another and who controls the release of materials and equipment should all be clearly described and understood.

Leaving the teaching room during a lesson is also a significant rite of passage. Which pupil has the biggest problem with bladder and bowels?

We have asked on countless occasions for pupils to bring a note from their doctor or parents regarding such problems. The consequence of such a request

has more often than not been a miraculous disap-
pearance of the symptoms!

How your class leaves the room at the end of a
lesson should be a pre-planned and controlled process.
Disorder or rowdiness on release from class can spoil
a good lesson. The parting impression pupils will have
is of your poor control.

There are many forms of release which can be
equally effective:

♦ letting them go one by one

♦ allowing those from the good table/row to leave first

♦ releasing the quietest pupils first

♦ letting everyone leave when the class is silent.

Stand by the door and if movement is appropriate give
quiet praise.

Aim to be creative about managing the movement of
pupils when they enter, leave and move around your
domain. Effective management of movement commu-
nicates clearly to all pupils, but especially to those with
EBD, that you are in charge.

Wall space

Walls are the clothing of the classroom. If they are
smart, tidy and up to date then they send out a strong
positive message. Walk around the school after the
pupils have gone home and see how classroom walls
appear to you. What do they say about the teacher, the

pupils and, taken as a collection, what do they say about the school?

It is often useful to dedicate a specific wall for a specific purpose. Maybe one for pupils' latest work, one focusing on a general subject area, and of course a wall especially for teaching.

The walls displaying pupils' work must always be up to date and smart, showing how much you respect their effort. Displaying work by an EBD pupil, if up to standard, can make the pupil feel included in the academic process of the class.

Your teaching wall should also be current, smart and stimulating. Pupils take note of walls and consciously or unconsciously relate them to your attitude to the job. This wall is an exciting area containing some of your communication aids. These can range from the glories of the interactive whiteboard to the old favourite, chalk and talk. Both have a place. Video can also be used. Overhead projectors can be helpful and, of course, the wonders of PowerPoint are almost unbeatable. Your teaching wall is your communication zone designed to stimulate and entrance pupils. The use of multimedia is clearly going to excite and educate pupils more than a dull, badly produced piece of photocopying. EBD pupils are far more likely to respond to exciting and stimulating images and consequently are going to see some advantage to paying attention. Remember, you are competing with television, the Internet, computer games and videos.

Furniture

To some teachers their desk is their security blanket, to others it is of little significance. Your desk and the decisions you make about it will say a lot about you as a person and a teacher:

♦ Is it the resource centre for the class or just for the teacher?

♦ Where do you place it and what role does it play?

♦ Do you sit behind, in front or even on top of it?

♦ What message is given out about its use?

♦ Do pupils queue to be seen, have their work marked? Does the queue form in front of the desk like a wall of bodies waiting for a free kick? If so, does this divide the teacher from the class?

♦ Are there planned routes to the desk or is it at the pupils' discretion when and how they arrive there?

Your desk is your base. Pupils will read aspects of your discipline from how you use your desk and what purpose it serves. This is especially true of our EBD friends, who would use a poorly positioned queue as a screen behind which to do untold and deviant things! Think about these things. They can affect your ability to teach the way you want to.

Think about spaces behind classroom furniture.

We once watched a pupil being physically assaulted behind a bookcase. The teacher (a very experienced professional) was completely unaware of the incident.

Problems can start away from your gaze in corners, behind cupboards, screens, walls and curtains. Sort these areas out, making the room as safe as possible. Make sure you can see every pupil at a glance and if you need them to see you, make sure all pupils can. Often with behaviour problems it's not how you respond to events that is important but how you prevent the trouble from starting in the first place.

Equipment

Often during a lesson you will need to use or give out equipment. If you make sure, before a lesson, that everything you need is to hand, working and available in the right quantities, you will save yourself a considerable amount of grief. Videos that don't work, having to send for additional equipment, leaving the room to get things you've forgotten, turning your back on the class to try to get your PowerPoint presentation to work or fetching something from the stock cupboard will all be nectar to your EBD pupils.

We have seen a dried-up felt-tip trigger a near riot and a non-functioning video machine lead to total chaos.

Rules for the classroom

Some people have a problem with the word 'rule', often preferring 'expectation'. We would lean more towards the former, as expectations can support rules and are a useful back up to them.

e.g.   Rule: We must all be ready to start the lesson on time.

31

> Expectation: We should be responsible for our own equipment.

The expectation makes the rule possible. One rule can have many expectations, therefore rules should be thought about carefully. The rules of the classroom should be made by all who take part in the lesson. The whole class should feel some ownership of them.

◆ There should be between five and, say, eight separate rules, the fewer the better.

◆ They should always be catchy, short and as positive as possible.

◆ Negotiate the content with all the pupils and any support assistants who are involved. Creative discussions can produce worthwhile rule setting.

◆ Make sure the discussions centre round delivering the curriculum. Don't get side-tracked onto things like where chewing gum should be put.

◆ Make sure the rules are environmentally specific and relate to the behaviours required. Avoid like the plague phrases such as 'We must all be nice to each other'. Rules must be real!

◆ Display the rules clearly and tidily. Damage or defacement must be repaired immediately. As a matter of course, rules should be kept alive by constantly being referred to.

◆ Perhaps the most important thing to remember is that rules should be kept fresh by being changed, adapted and discussed on a regular basis. It is hard to do but well worth the struggle.

Learning Support Assistants, Teaching Assistants and volunteers

In today's school climate, with the emphasis on inclusion, you will often have support staff in your classroom. They may be attached to specific pupils with special needs or supporting the whole class, or you may have volunteer parents/grandparents offering assistance.

These adults can make a considerable difference to your ability to deliver the curriculum and their contribution can be both positive and negative, depending on how you manage them.

Keep in mind that these adults can be:

♦ from very varied backgrounds

♦ bringing with them a variety of skills

♦ very confident/greatly lacking in confidence

♦ bossy/timid

♦ working with a specific child, often a very challenging one

♦ supporting the whole group

♦ paid/volunteers.

Your role in managing these adults

Bear in mind that the classroom is your domain and that you are ultimately in charge. Build a positive relationship with support staff. Work hard to respect and value them, finding time to talk to them about their work. Work in partnership with them but direct them clearly.

Summary

Your teaching room is your domain and the stage on which you teach. The way you manage the space can be of great benefit or considerable detriment to the learning which takes place in your lessons. EBD pupils in particular will find the holes in your design and management.

Here is a quick checklist to work through:

The room

1. Can you cut out external distraction?

2. Are you aware of the danger spots?

3. Can you engineer the seating plan to reduce potential trouble spots?

4. Do you surround challenging pupils with settled ones?

5. Can you see all pupils at all times?

Mobility

1. Do you admit and release classes in good order?

2. Are pathways described?

3. Is the best use made of floor space?

4. Do you control entrances and exits?

5. Is your mobility fit for purpose?

Walls

1. Are wall displays attractive?

2. Are the displays current?

3. Is pupils' recent work displayed?

4. Is your teaching wall interesting, varied and smart?

Your desk

1. Does its placement assist in the maintenance of good order?

2. Do you hide behind it or can you teach away from it?

Storage units

1. Do they create hidden corners?

2. If they need to be used, are they easily accessible?

Equipment

1. Do you check that it is working before the lesson?

2. Do you have the correct number/amount of everything you need?

Rules

1. Are all the rules fresh?

2. Do you have less than eight of them?

3. Are they positively phrased?

4. Are they fit for purpose?

5. Have they been agreed by all?

If you are able to thoughtfully engineer both the social and the physical dynamics of your teaching room your chances of successfully delivering your lesson to all pupils, but especially those with EBD, will be considerably enhanced.

4

EBD Pupils' Learning

The most effective therapy we as teachers can offer our troubled pupils is to make them feel academically successful and part of a well-behaved school. Pupils with Emotional and Behavioural Difficulties generally do seem to find learning of any kind very difficult. Throughout our joint teaching experience of seventy years we have always been amazed at the resistance to learning that pupils with EBD seem to hold dear. They appear to have a map of learning designed for another planet. They can find remembering the yearly seasons in the correct order difficult but can recall events from years ago in fine detail.

A colleague of ours returned to his old school after being away for 18 months abroad and on meeting a pupil he was asked what he had done with the blue and yellow tie he had taken off at his teacher's final assembly as a symbol of leaving teaching. The pupil in question in Year 5 could hardly read, could not remember the days of the week and needed concrete aids to do basic addition and subtraction. He went on to relate in detail many behaviours of his old teacher, even down to what he liked and disliked for lunch.

Emotional and Behavioural Difficulties

We have encountered EBD pupils who were academically bright and quick to learn, bright enough to go on to university, but in general the academic performance of the EBD pupils we taught was low.

Why are these pupils so resistant to learning? There are many questions we should ask.

♦ Do some pupils have a specific learning difficulty such as dyslexia, which colours their view of school and being successful there?

♦ Do they develop learning difficulties as a result of their EBD?

♦ Does early negative experience of school create a resistance to academic learning throughout their school life?

♦ Do pupils who do not experience what is described as good enough parenting (Winnicott, 1964) find relating to other pupils, adults and rules in school very difficult?

♦ Does the social isolation caused by EBD create a resentment of the social norms expected in school?

♦ Do these pupils fight back against the rules of the school as a result of high or low self-esteem?

♦ Do some pupils have such a multitude of disabilities that mainstream schooling is virtually impossible?

The danger is in believing that there is only one cause of their learning difficulties. We should keep an open mind about why they don't learn as well or as quickly as their peers and make sure appropriate assessments are, or have been, undertaken in all areas which appear problematic.

We might need to look closely at one or several of the following:

♦ eyesight – all manner of problems, including short-sightedness, blurred or double vision, amblyopia ('lazy eye'), crossed eyes

♦ hearing – glue ear, partial deafness

♦ dyslexia – it may be a cause not a consequence

♦ dyscalculia – again, could be a cause

♦ dyspraxia – fine and gross motor difficulties

♦ epilepsy – small absences not previously observed

♦ attention difficulties (ADHD)

♦ the autistic spectrum

♦ speech and language.

There could be other factors which seriously impact on a pupil's ability to learn, such as high levels of anxiety caused by abuse inside or outside the family.

It is only by objective and detailed analysis of the possible causes of a pupil's learning difficulties that we can begin to design appropriate remedial pro-grammes. The clarity, efficiency and sensitivity of the SEN systems in your school will be fundamental to this process.

In our special school the majority of pupils, on admission, were seriously below the academic and social norms for their age groups. They exhibited little ability, or willingness, to acquire skills which would enhance their understanding of their physical/social world. This lack of curiosity was at times breathtaking. It was as if they had sealed themselves in against all danger or, as more often seemed the case, they believed they 'knew enough'.

We recently attended a staff meeting in a large mainstream school and were struck by how weary the teachers appeared. One comment on beheviour which came towards the end of the meeting summed up the whole complexity of teaching pupils with EBD: 'If you give them something to colour in, trace round, or fill in then you can have a nice quiet lesson. Try to give them more challenging work and they don't want to know and you get trouble.'

The key to success with learning is lowering pupils' stress through clever curriculum design and delivery carefully tailored to accommodate their specific learning difficulties. When teaching these pupils keep in mind their fragile academic self-esteem and their poor social skills. Any kind of real or perceived slight to their competence can have serious consequences.

In many ways pupils with EBD are no different from your regular pupils. All will be more engaged in learning if your lessons are interesting and you make good use of video, computers, whiteboards, practical demonstrations, whole-class activities, group work and individual work, to vary the pace and focus of your lessons. However, there are a number of essential musts you need to have in your repertoire if you want to see your EBD pupils make significant progress with their learning.

♦ As they often suffer from attention difficulties, tasks set must be relatively short, clearly stated and achievable.

♦ Learning must be reinforced by repetition and practice.

♦ The books and equipment you give them must be smart. A torn book, bent spoon, or cracked instrument will be perceived as a personal slight.

♦ Differentiation must be covert. They will not accept work which they perceive as 'babyish', condescending or different from that given to their classmates.

♦ The seating position of the pupil must be planned carefully to ensure the minimum amount of distraction. Near the front works well.

♦ Overt academic put-down must not happen. For example, don't ask them to read aloud if you know they will struggle.

♦ Genuine success in terms of good work and/or behaviour must be instantly rewarded even if it's just with quiet praise.

♦ Integrate any specific recommendations regarding the pupil into your lesson planning.

Group work

Group work should be approached tentatively. These pupils often find group work and turn taking difficult. Pair work with a sensible and understanding partner may be a preferred option. Of course we want our EBD pupils to become more socially competent, but for them group work is a powder keg waiting to ignite. Move towards group work with caution and socially engineer the groups to ensure settled learning. Co-opting understanding and friendly classmates into 'a circle of friends' to give subtle support to the pupil can be a very successful strategy.

Praise and rewards

Giving praise when earned and rewarding positive steps, either in terms of academic attainment or in attitude and behaviour, are essential elements of working with EBD pupils. Some will accept individually tailored reward systems while others will respond more positively to class- and school-based systems. The essential thing to remember is that rewards support and reinforce pupils' learning. This is a key strategy.

Flexibility

Schools which are flexible tend to be more successful with their EBD pupils. What is the point of insisting a pupil does PE when he/she has always become seriously stressed about changing. This stress may be related to sexual/physical abuse. During these lessons he/she may be better employed, say helping in the library.

For one pupil on a reintegration programme to a secondary school, French was creating huge difficulties. We managed to acquire funding for a computer and software specifically for him. Instead of French he went to Learning Support and did individual work on his computer, improving his numeracy and literacy skills. His behaviour improved and he successfully completed mainstream schooling.

Schools should always have learning as their primary focus. They must describe clearly techniques and support systems which are in place to maximize all pupils' learning potential.

Flexible individual programmes as identified through the SEN process are described in more detail in Chapter 6.

Information and Communication Technology (ICT)

EBD pupils can benefit considerably from the use of ICT as it provides a non-threatening environment in which to achieve success. For many, using the computer presents a calm setting in which they are controlling the pace and level of work. It can help them to tackle writing tasks with more confidence and they are able to produce work that looks very competent. Of course, ICT must not be your only strategy for engaging EBD pupils in learning. It can circumvent the whole spectrum of human interaction which they find so difficult. However, its perceived high status, its flexibility, the ever improving software, its privacy and ability to aid self-expression for pupils with poor literacy skills make ICT an especially valuable learning tool.

Involving parents

The parents of EBD children often have their own history of failure at school and can be school phobic.

Schools who work hard to engage parents in their pupils' learning are more likely to see these pupils progress.

Jed was not settled in school and consequently was not learning. His mum, who was herself aggressive and challenging, was invited in to spend the morning in his class. She reluctantly agreed. Jed responded by working really hard to impress his mum and his mum became engaged in his learning. For Jed and his mum this was a turning point.

Summary

Many EBD pupils experience learning difficulties. Their failure to learn effectively can be caused by a multitude of factors, but the main presenting characteristics are low academic self-esteem and high stress levels in the learning situation.

They can and will learn if schools are sensitive to their special educational needs. Schools with well-organized and varied curriculum delivery, strong SEN support and parent liaison, a culture of praise and inclusion and a recognition that flexibility is a key to success are the most likely to be successful in helping these pupils to learn.

5

Your Basic Skills

Pupils with EBD are hugely sensitive to the actions and attitudes of the adults and pupils in their classes.

This chapter will give teachers a repertoire of techniques which will maximize their chances of managing their more difficult pupils. Think of it as learning a new sport, a musical instrument or even a new foreign language. It can be challenging and fun.

These techniques include the use of:

♦ positive language

♦ scanning

♦ interventions

♦ body posture, facial expression and voice.

The classroom is your stage and these skills can widen your ability to deliver the right line at the right time with the right amount of impact.

Positive language

Try positive language as an experiment out of school. Talk positively all the time to whoever you meet in whatever situation and see what effect it can have. Don't overdo it, you might be sectioned!

Try out positive language in an interaction with someone you know reasonably well. See how a number of positive remarks, praise for action and saying thank you for support can change the dynamic. Try remarks like:

'Good to see you'

'Like your hair'

'You look well'

'Thanks again for the other evening, I really enjoyed myself'

'What a lovely flat you have'

'Nice to meet your partner, what a nice chap'

'I read the book you recommended and really enjoyed it'.

We first came across this in the USA. The head of a school for extremely disturbed and at times dangerous young men took us round. Every pupil he met he greeted with great enthusiasm (shaking hands), praised them for some aspect of their behaviour or clothing, or referred to a previous event with warmth. The pupils reacted with obvious pleasure and beamed with appreciation. The whole school used this warm positive attitude, thus disarming the pupils and making them feel valued.

Transfer this to your classroom and see how the mood changes and pupils respond. Welcome them as they enter. Don't be involved in sorting books, cleaning boards and moving furniture; these should all have been done already. Greet pupils at the door, direct them with a smile and wherever possible make positive remarks:

'Hi', 'how you doing?', 'good day'

'Good to see you' (even if it isn't!)

'Like your hair' (shoes, coat, bag – whatever you can find to praise)

'Good work last week. Just marked it. Well done'

'I like this class, so many nice kids'.

Then keep it going: 'Well done for settling down', 'you have nearly all put your bags under the desk', as opposed to 'how many more times do I have to tell you?' Obviously too many! Being positive wherever possible keeps the mood upbeat and buoyant. Where you see a chance to praise, particularly EBD pupils, do it. Many of them don't get praised very often and rarely perceive the classroom as a theatre of achievement.

Look to speak positively at all times, seeking out behaviours to praise, work to celebrate and pupils to congratulate. An example of this is date writing at the top of the page. 'Where's the date?' can be restated as 'great start, but it would be even better with the date at the top'. This is not rocket science. You are simply reinforcing good behaviour as opposed to rewarding bad behaviour by constantly drawing attention to it. You know the phrases to avoid:

- 'stop doing that'
- 'be quiet'
- 'how many more times?'
- 'get out'
- 'shut up'
- 'move now'.

There is a time and place for such aggressive remarks but they should be few and far between, not setting the mood of the classroom. You should aim for your classroom to be a positive, work-centred and successful environment. Count up your positive and negative remarks and see which ones you use the most. Work hard to make positive remarks four times as frequently as negative. If you watch the most successful teachers they do it without thinking.

Scanning

This is your key skill. Without it you are like a passenger aircraft flying over the middle of the Atlantic without radar or radio.

Scanning is not complicated. It simply involves running your eyes constantly over the whole class. In our EBD school we expected teachers to check the class every 10 to 20 seconds. This time interval is about right for a new class, but gradually as you get to know behaviour, scanning can be less frequent.

Wherever you are in the classroom, gym, art room, lab, every 20 seconds or so check what all the pupils are doing. This simple, easy process can prevent the escalation of serious behaviours by catching them before they develop. It can prevent undesirable movement by monitoring who is where and with whom. It displays to the most difficult pupils that you are up front and aware. Some pupils respond by feeling secure and therefore staying calm. Others see that trying it on is not going to be successful.

Visual scanning gives information on the following:

♦ *Current state of whole-class behaviour:* You can monitor the quality of your teaching and the suitability of the work given. How many pupils are on task? Is the equipment a help or hindrance to the progress of the lesson?

♦ *Individual children's activities:* You can constantly check your most difficult pupils. What are they doing? Who are they talking to? Do they understand the work given? Can they do it?

♦ *Developing difficult behaviour:* You can spot behaviours that are developing between specific pupils, identify the root causes and how many pupils are involved. It enables you to understand the specific nature of the challenging behaviour and make an informed judgement before intervening.

♦ *Effects of specific management methods:* You can check on the effects of your management methods. Did anyone listen? Was it the right instruction by you? How did pupils react? Was it good for the mental health of the class and how did our EBD pupils react? If you don't check on the consequences of your own behaviour you are not going to develop as the lively creative teacher we're sure you want to be!

♦ *The instigators of specific incidents:* You can identify those responsible for bullying, breakages, verbal abuse, etc.

By scanning and keeping a constant eye on the likely hot spots you will be able to respond to difficult behaviour and its consequences with sound knowledge and a good history of the incident. 'It wasn't me sir' can be responded to accurately and if you are confident, which you should be, with a smile. You are in the driving seat, on top and feeling good.

Auditory scanning

Listening to the noise of the class can give you some idea of the mood of individuals, small groups and the whole class. Keep your ears wide open for noises that pre-empt trouble.

The tone of voice/voices (e.g. noisy verbal interchange; silly, slightly over the top laughter; sharp angry speaking; a sudden lull in noise) and the movement of objects and furniture (e.g. desks slamming; chairs being pushed; doors opening/closing) can all indicate a mood or be leading to an undesirable action. Catching things in the bud can save you an enormous amount of work later.

Make scanning part of your life in the classroom. After a while it becomes second nature because, just like your pupils, if you behave in a certain way and you are rewarded, you continue to do it. In fact, you tend to do it more often and become more proficient at it.

We were once involved in a series of in-service training sessions with a group of teachers in a tough city upper school and during one session were extolling the virtues of scanning. The following week a teacher on the course said how exhausted he was by scanning. The technique had worked very well with his classes who were much quieter, better behaved and more on task. However, he concentrated so hard on scanning that even when watching TV at home he found himself constantly scanning his well-behaved, rather bewildered children!

Interventions

Interventions are markers the teacher lays down for the class, bringing together scanning and positive talking. The teacher moves the class along, guiding them on the desirable route.

Interventions can be grouped into three types: positive, preventative and necessary. They all require knowledge of the class, the individuals that make up the more difficult elements, and your own knowledge of your capabilities.

Positive interventions

For individuals
This is positive language in action. The teacher identifies good behaviour, good work, good on-task behaviour and responds positively.

With individual pupils you can say things like 'fantastic', 'well done', 'brilliant', 'great piece of work', 'let's show it to the whole class', each rewarding phrase related to what works for an individual pupil. Some pupils prefer a very quiet 'that's great, keep it up' whispered in their ear, or even just a gentle non-verbal thumbs up.

You must catch EBD pupils getting it right and praise them. Use praise as the carrot. You would be surprised how many pupils love positive, rewarding words and gestures from their teacher.

If you want to reinforce good work/behaviour use individual praise. 'Well done, Tom; you're working brilliantly' can have a remarkable effect on other pupils sitting nearby. Observe the rest straightening their backs when you say 'Sit up please. Thank you, Susan.'

Just one word of warning: do not praise what is not worthy; the pupils will smell a rat.

For small groups

Working the class as a number of small groups is not easy to manage. Each group will take on its own character, some good, some not so good. Positive interventions need to be regular, clear and supportive of good behaviour. Phrases such as 'you have worked well as a group', 'this group is producing outstanding work' and 'what a quiet, hard-working bunch' encourage positive momentum.

Praise indicating a reward can be effective. 'Looks as if this group will be able to leave first' and 'this group will definitely go on the field trip' indicates to others that there is a consequence for good behaviour.

When a class is split into small groups discipline can be difficult. Some group members interact badly. Remember that pupils with EBD have poor social skills. By using the positive phrase/remark to other groups you bring pressure to bear on the disruptive pupil from members of their group who are deprived of praise. Regrouping can be a solution (splitting up difficult pupils or pupils that don't like each other), but also giving treats and preferences to groups working well can often change attitudes of other groups in the class.

For the whole class
In terms of discipline, whole-class teaching, with everyone facing the front, is the easiest to manage. For your introduction the class is lined up in front of you. You are centre stage and you can see every eye looking at you. When the class begins work you are free to roam as you see fit. Positive remarks and phrases help you signal what you want and enable you to express your appreciation for good work and atti-tude. Walking around saying things like 'good working atmosphere in here', 'you lot are good to teach', 'I am enjoying this lesson', 'much better behaviour than last week' and 'you are quiet, I like that; it makes teaching worthwhile' all signal your strong approval of the class.

A positive intervention with the whole class keeps the momentum going. Pupils sense that they are part of a good tribe, getting it right and being successful. If the feel-good atmosphere is referred to on a regular basis some of the difficult pupils won't want to oppose the successful tribe; instead they will seek to be a part of it.

Preventative interventions

These interventions are subtle and require more precision. The teacher sees a situation developing and intervenes to prevent escalation. These interventions tend not always to be positive, but be aware that aggressive intervention can cause serious escalation. Here are some examples:

'You have worked well so far. Perhaps you are tired and need to sit quietly?'

'I will come and see you in a minute, looks good from here'

'It might be a good idea to start that part of the task again'

'Which of these fresh tasks would you like to start?'

'Perhaps I got the groups wrong and next time we need to separate you two?'

You are redirecting but using positive phrases such as 'worked well', 'good idea', 'fresh task', 'would you like to' and the tone is clear and directive. Your voice has to be clear, positive but firm. Even a bit of carefully thought out humour might just ease the situation.

Some behaviour settles without any intervention; eye contact and awareness is all that is required. Some behaviour doesn't always settle immediately but slowly subsides. Good teachers allow 'take-up time'. You can often avoid a confrontation by giving sufficient time for pupils to calm down, regroup and behave in an appropriate way. This enables them to preserve their delicate ego.

A colleague went to Dan's class to take him to his mainstream school. He was anxious about going and refused, saying 'I'm not f***ing going'. The teacher just said quietly, 'That could make our life a bit difficult. Maybe think about it while I go and pick up some files' and went away for several minutes, thus giving him take-up time. When she returned Dan was ready to come with her.

Other preventative interventions can be directed towards the work set and the responsibility of the whole class to stay on task:

'I thought we had agreed to do it this way?'

'I don't think the class would be happy with that behaviour'

'We are all losing time with this behaviour'

'We're not going to get finished today and we're all going to lose points'.

Notice the use of 'we' and 'the class'. This uses the power of the group and group desires and aspirations to de-escalate developing difficult situations. EBD pupils feel the pressure from the class to stay on task. These interventions are work orientated and surround the need for compliance. Often disruption can be a consequence of attention-seeking behaviour, but by requesting a general compliance you are marking demanding behaviour as undesirable without directly confronting and risking escalation.

Necessary interventions

These are required when preventative interventions are not having the desired effect. If behaviour reaches a level where teaching is becoming difficult, then firmer interventions are essential. Behaviour can be like a wood fire. Once it reaches a certain temperature it will burn anything (serious behaviours are discussed in Chapter 8). You are beginning to lose control of your stage. It is important to get your words right and act clearly. Any slip can escalate the problem.

Our EBD pupils know who, or what, is driving the undesirable behaviour. If you have been scanning correctly then you will have some knowledge of the antecedents and be aware of the dynamics. If you have not been scanning then you run the risk of choosing badly and hurtling down the slide into the abyss.

What can you do?

You can choose the most amenable member of the challenging group and direct him/her firmly and clearly:

'OK, back to work please'

'Enough, thank you. Get on with . . .' (specify precisely the task)

'Stop; back to work please'

'You move over here please'

The last one is a high-risk strategy because if it does not work you are in deep trouble, which is why I suggest you first select the pupil you are most confident of managing.

The language is different from that used in the previous interventions. There is no compromise, no positives, just clear direction, short and sweet, but no shouting. If you shout you are fanning the flames and losing credibility. By bringing about a change of behaviour in one member of the group the rest will often subside, particularly if a few firm and knowing looks are given. 'Please' and 'thank you' are optional. We have always used them because, even in difficult situations, respect and good manners must still be evident.

If the intervention is not working with the most amenable of the negative sub-group then you have to go for the pupil or pupils who are causing the problem and/or the whole sub-group. This is a delicate process and needs careful consideration. Everything you say counts and will be listened to by all class members.

You need to be physically close to the centre of the difficulties. The pupils have to smell your calm, healthy presence. Your voice has to be clear and steady, your tone completely confident, regardless of how you feel inside. Your posture should be straight and solid and your facial expression calm. The interventions should all be work related and direct. This intervention is at its most difficult when you are facing a new class. Of the interventions listed below it is sensible to select the one that most readily fits your personality and teaching style.

♦ 'Could everyone stop work, sit up and face me (*wait*). Right, let's start again.'

♦ Sit down in the middle of the trouble and express an interest in the work. Ask them what they don't understand. Often your close, unthreatening presence can calm the whole thing down.

♦ Stand in front of the whole class and acquire silence. Restate the lesson target and reiterate the class rules. 'Off we go again.'

♦ Alter the pace of the lesson by changing the activity from passive to active or vice versa. Move pupils to different seating arrangements.

♦ Just stand close and perhaps behind the troubled ones. Do all your teaching and management over their heads, with the occasional remark about your wish for their compliance. Often they will get so sick and tired of your presence they will shut up and get on out of a sense of self-preservation. You have taken back the territory.

As you can see, the interventions above are not directed straight at the problem pupil. This is called 'vector therapy' and involves persuading in the right direction.

Warning

The following teacher behaviours can lead to increased disruption:

♦ responding too quickly to difficulties

♦ lacking defusing skills

♦ direct confrontation, leaving pupils few options

♦ being inconsistent classroom managers

♦ being subjective regarding pupils' difficulties

♦ excessive and/or continuous shouting at an individual pupil or a class

♦ persistent and targeted negative responses to individuals and/or groups

♦ over-familiarity of a sexual or personal nature with individual pupils (this can include flirting)

♦ talking about pupils' problems and behaviour in front of them

♦ humiliating pupils in front of their peers

♦ collusion of any kind: against another adult's decision; against a school expectation; in favour of one pupil against another.

Body posture, facial expression and voice

How you stand, walk about, sit and how you dress sends out strong messages to pupils about you, how you respect them, how you think about your work and the whole process of teaching.

Standing straight and tall, walking quietly, maintaining a quiet body when things are difficult in the classroom all send out the right signals to the class and especially to EBD pupils who monitor any sign of frailty. I am certain they can smell the first bead of sweat as it appears on your flesh.

Teachers also need to manage facial expressions with care and consideration. Charles Darwin (1999 [1872]) wrote extensively on facial expression. He suggested that we inherited our facial expressions from our distant ancestors and as we evolved so did our facial expressions; it is that fundamental.

He also suggested that the interpretation of the meanings behind the basic human facial expressions is universal. Therefore facial expressions and the reading of pupils' faces are crucial to sound management of the classroom.

You need to analyse your face and how you express emotion. Do you smile a lot/little? Do you furrow your brow and turn down your mouth? Do you close your eyes when you speak? Do you show your teeth when you shout? Have a good long look in the mirror and see what your pupils see. What do you think?

Facial expressions coupled with body posture are vital not just to your delivery of the curriculum but to how you are seen as a person.

Facial expressions can be used to change the mood of the classroom. They can be very effective as a non-verbal warning to a pupil or as a tool for celebrating good behaviour. A smile with a thumbs up can be as good as a star or twenty ticks.

Your face as you greet pupils can set the whole mood of the first part of a lesson. A smiling face and a cheerful word can get the whole day off to a good start. Shaking your head and frowning slightly can reduce silly behaviour quite quickly. Furrowing your brow and shaking your head can work wonders with a difficult group, without you even saying a single word.

Try this: When you get home after school, play a short game, say for thirty minutes, with whoever you live with. Agree not to speak, and communicate only with non-verbal signals. You will be amazed at how quickly your face becomes very animated. A bit like us trying to be understood in a foreign country through an elaborate use of hand gestures and facial expressions!

We once did a whole assembly in our EBD school without speaking a single word and without giving any prior warning to the pupils. We were amazed by how quickly they caught on, how easily they understood non-verbal communication and how well behaved they were.

◦ If you add to body posture and facial expression the clever and appropriate use of voice, you have a powerful clutch of skills. Spend a bit of time listening to people in public places and see how they use their voice to gain attention, win arguments, accept defeat and project themselves as a person. Go and listen to a good teacher and see how he/she uses the voice as a tool to manage pupils. A good strong tone, which is consistent, clearly understood and preferably without affectation, helps. Do you remember how you took the mickey out of teachers who had funny little quirks and pronounced some words very oddly?

Try to speak as quietly as you can when managing the class. This signals confidence and security. Speaking quietly also gives you scope to raise your voice. Just a slight increase in volume is noted by pupils as a marker. Stopping speaking in the middle of a sentence: 'Could we all please . . . be quiet' can be effective.

Coughs, 'shhhh' and 'Oh yes!', said quietly, can also have the desired effect. Short, sharp, sudden changes in pitch can lift pupils' heads and the speed at which you speak can have a significant effect on the listening potential of your EBD pupils.

Use your voice to the full. See it as a tool and make it work.

Summary

This chapter has discussed the use of key basic skills in the classroom, from positive language through scanning, interventions and finally the use of face, voice and body.

These are not intended to be used as separate skills but together to effectively manage all pupils but particularly those with EBD. If the use and development of such skills is seen as a challenge rather than a chore then they can significantly improve your teaching. Without that interest, creativity and zest for learning, you might become a teacher who, dare we say, deserves some of the awful behaviour you get?

Here is a checklist you might like to look over. Which of these positive physical/verbal characteristics do you possess?

Body language

♦ Assertively positive

♦ Standing tall

♦ Calm stance and facial expression

♦ Pleasant

♦ Calm and confident movement to all areas of the teaching space

♦ Non-threatening

- Non-confrontational

- Sensitive to the space between teacher/student (distance, level).

Use of voice

- Clear, quiet voice

- Effective use of pause

- Pleasant

- Some humour

- Sudden change of pitch, volume, tempo

- Anger used sparingly, after considerable positive input and in a calculated way

- Being a good listener as well as a good talker.

6

Your Place in the Whole-school Structure

Your workplace is your school. It is our experience that there are key whole-school factors which, if in place, will help you, the teacher, to work more successfully with all pupils but especially those with EBD.

The head teacher

The head teacher can be pivotal in a school, providing the drive and the direction for pupils and teachers alike. Outcomes are better when the head teacher shows firm leadership (Rutter *et al.*, 1979). 'What mattered was purposeful leadership' (Mortimore, 1987).

A mainstream school is an amalgam of complex populations of pupils, multi-disciplinary human resources, demanding legal and administrative systems and you the teacher. A strong head teacher who has a grasp of this complexity and who gathers round a competent and loyal staff team will make a great difference. It's a very tough job.

Buildings

The school buildings must be attractive, well managed and smart. Graffiti should be removed immediately as it often encourages further graffiti and small holes become craters.

In our special school, if a pupil kicked a hole in a wall, defaced a surface, or deliberately broke a window, the repair was always carried out as soon as possible with the pupil assisting and paying for some of the damage. This firm consequence directly related to action ensured that the school was always a clean, attractive and desirable place to be.

Furniture, equipment and décor

A clean school, attractive carpets (they reduce noise very significantly), smart furniture, well-painted halls, teaching rooms, corridors and toilets, and interesting, pupil-centred wall displays will all contribute to good behaviour. They help all pupils to feel respected and valued.

A dirty, poorly decorated school with few celebrations of pupils' achievements can easily give rise to 'don't care' and 'why should I?' feelings in pupils.

We once experienced a phase of major arguments, including fights, caused by pupils identifying a particular style of dining room chair as superior to the rest. Pupils who sat on lesser chairs were thought of as inferior. The mayhem was only solved when we threw away the motley collection of seating (which had acquired, in the pupils' eyes, a pecking order) and bought a set of identical blue chairs. Neither staff nor pupils were permitted to bring any other sort of chair into the dining room. Lunchtimes became much quieter.

The school grounds and whole-school mobility

Free association times can create more behaviour problems than the rest of the school day put together. There should always be staff monitoring movement around the school both between lessons and at breaktimes, including at least one senior staff member. Lunchtime is particularly hazardous and schools need to think very clearly about its benefits to the pupils. EBD pupils simply do not possess the social skills to manage the excessive mobility and social interaction which occurs, therefore good organization and staffing at this time are crucial. Systems for eating should be clear and dinner supervisors must be well trained in managing groups of pupils and should command respect.

'Letting off steam' in the lunch hour is often a misnomer for open warfare. Schools which shorten the lunchtime and finish the day earlier, with extra-curricular activities after school, can be better behaved.

Off-site activity in school hours should be directed and carefully monitored. We have visited mainstream schools where 'out of sight, out of mind' was often a philosophy; one which always haunts the user sooner rather than later.

Managing and evaluating behaviour: a whole-school approach

Rules and expectations

Your school will have a whole-school behaviour policy which has been discussed and agreed by staff, parents and pupils. This policy will clearly state the school rules and expectations and should be understood and supported by all.

The school's policy towards involving parents is particularly crucial when managing the behaviour of EBD pupils.

Rewards

In our work in mainstream schools we found that the pupils identified as the most disruptive were fully aware of the consequences of poor behaviour, but had little or no knowledge of whole-school reward systems.

An ethos of all staff catching and rewarding good behaviour is a much more effective way of working than constantly growling, particularly with challenging pupils. Positive is infinitely more therapeutic than negative.

The school's reward system needs to be significant, current and owned and understood by all pupils and staff. The school council is an effective forum for designing and reviewing systems of reward. This pupil ownership is vital. Imposed systems have much less clout with today's more assertive youngsters.

Incident recording

However well organized your school, it is inevitable that you will have to manage challenging behaviour. Recording these behaviours clearly and following them up is one of the most effective and precise tools available to you.

Emotional and Behavioural Difficulties

Schools should have a centrally managed incident-recording system. All staff and pupils, especially EBD pupils, should be aware of the implications of the school's incident-recording system and its consequences. Prompt and accurate recording of behaviours identified by all as unacceptable gives schools current, concrete evidence of the frequency, severity and location of the behaviours. This is essential information for the support of pupils with SEN, especially EBD, as it enables the school to identify the causes, frequency and severity of their difficulties and tailor the interventions appropriately.

Teachers should record all incidents which prevent the curriculum from being delivered or which create problems outside the classroom. The criteria used should be understood and agreed by all staff. Whole-staff fairness and consistency in incident recording is essential if it is to be an effective management tool. Staff involvement in the differentiation of the severity of incidents should be a significant part of continuing in-service training.

A graded system of recording incidents clarifies the weighting placed on behaviour of a specific kind, enabling the teacher to score the seriousness of the behaviour. Four levels would help to identify the degree of difficulty of the presenting behaviour.

Level	Behaviour
Level 1	◆ Swearing ◆ Answering back ◆ Out of seat ◆ Constantly making noises

Level 2	◆ Verbal abuse to another pupil ◆ Continuous swearing ◆ Refusing work ◆ Preventing the teacher speaking to the whole class
Level 3	◆ Verbal abuse to an adult ◆ Refusing to leave the classroom ◆ Refusing to obey reasonable requests ◆ Assault on another pupil ◆ Leaving the classroom without permission
Level 4	◆ Verbally and/or physically threatening an adult ◆ Assault on an adult ◆ Leaving the school grounds without permission ◆ Possession of illegal substances ◆ A violent attack on another pupil

Question: would you place the behaviour described above in the same levels?

All difficult and oppositional behaviour should have a consequence in school which is fair and relevant. This consequence should be an expression to the pupil of disapproval but must have reparation and reconciliation as its focus. Punishment *per se* only breeds resentment and alienation. Schools need to look honestly at the outcomes of detention on the most frequent users.

Exclusions

On occasions, a pupil will have such a severe crisis that the school feels it must exclude him/her for a fixed term. This should be viewed as an extreme response and used by schools with great caution. Often the consequences of exclusion are:

Emotional and Behavioural Difficulties

♦ notoriety

♦ alienation of pupil and parent

♦ cementing the pupil's connections with the community's negative sub-groups

♦ increased drug taking

♦ crime.

Most of all it immediately shelves the problem, delays resolution and rewards challenging behaviour.

Perhaps a better solution following a serious breakdown in discipline would be for the pupil to be in school, separated from all inappropriate contact and directed to repairing the damage caused, or for the school to have an exchange agreement with another school for off-site time out.

The following are some successful strategies we have used.

Behaviour	Consequence
Bullying	A pupil making something for the pupil bullied or helping the victim in some way
Abuse of staff	Helping staff with their day-to-day work
Verbal abuse of a dinner lady	Helping in some way with the preparation of meals (we can hear the horns of risk assessment blowing loud and clear)
Damage to property	Involve the pupil in putting it right and repairing the damage
Drug abuse, including smoking	Have projects prepared for pupils to complete about the dangers of all forms of drug abuse before they are permitted to join the main body of the school again

We are aware that all these responses are labour intensive and require more creative thinking than exclusions. However, the outcome of immediate reparation is far more likely to reduce the overall need for resources in the long term, as the connection between behaviour and consequence is clear to the pupils.

Permanent exclusions remove the pupil from his/her only continuous connection with the neighbourhood and by doing so ends any hope of adequate resolution. As a consequence the pupil is often lost as a contributor to our society for quite some time.

At our EBD school we decided as a staff to adopt a no exclusion (both fixed term and permanent) policy. There was a strong feeling that by excluding pupils we were punishing them for their SEN. Rather like excluding a child with dyslexia for not being able to read Shakespeare. Over the final four years of our work the school did not have a single exclusion, fixed term or permanent. There was an improvement in general behaviour and a significant drop in seriously challenging behaviour.

The Special Educational Needs Code of Practice 2001

The Code of Practice has accepted the growing prevalence of EBD among our school population and given it clear recognition as a disability. EBD is now recognized as coming under the umbrella of SEN, which is very good news for these troubled children. The Code's staged approach to supporting a pupil's SEN gives schools a clear structure for managing even the most difficult and challenging pupils with a differentiated and successful repertoire of responses.

Figure 6.1 illustrates how the structure of the Code of Practice (DfES, 2001) should work as a continuous thread, supporting pupils through all the phases of schooling. Pupils can move up and down through the SEN action levels depending on their level of adjustment. This is particularly relevant to those with EBD,

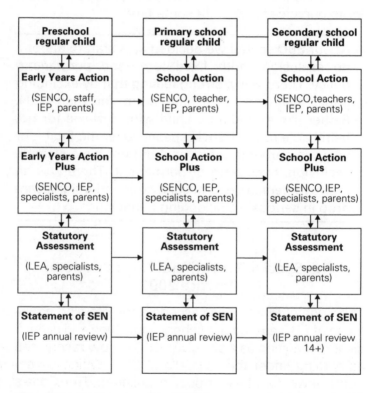

Fig. 6.1. Pathways for SEN interventions in school

who can move from well adjusted to difficult to almost impossible and back to adjusted depending on both internal and external factors. This helps us to achieve the aim of providing them with the least restrictive environment they can successfully manage.

A brief description of the staged levels of intervention and various responsibilities

The teacher

If you are concerned about a pupil you should keep an individual pupil log, enabling you to maintain a dated record of all dealings with the pupil, the pupil's parents and external agencies. Make notes of all conversations, including telephone calls with the pupil's parents and anyone concerned with the pupil's difficulties. This is particularly important for EBD pupils living, as they often do, complex and sometimes chaotic lives. Talk to your Special Educational Needs Co-ordinator (SENCO), or a member of your Senior Management Team (SMT), about pupils who are causing you concern and describe clearly and objectively their difficulties.

The SENCO and SMT are responsible for the day-to-day operation of the SEN policy. They co-ordinate provision through School Action, offering interventions which are additional to or different from those provided as part of the school's usual differentiated curriculum and strategies.

School Action

It is only when a pupil is unable to be contained within the normal boundaries of the school's differentiated academic and social systems that 'School Action' is considered. This big step is taken when the pupil's behaviour is persistently preventing learning either for the pupil or for the class, or for both. It is at this point that your recorded observations and rigorous noting of incidents will be invaluable as evidence of the pupil's special needs. A School Action intervention requires the involvement of the head teacher and/or the SMT, the SENCO and the parents. It is at this stage that an Individual Education Plan (IEP) is written.

The IEP must contain:

♦ a clear analysis of the pupil's SEN

♦ clear and meaningful targets in relation to the progress we would all like to see

♦ a detailed plan of how the targets are to be achieved

♦ a time-scale for progress

♦ the identification of additional support, e.g. mentor, key teacher, Learning Support Assistant, Educational Social Worker (ESW).

You should be aware of the work undertaken by ESWs, who allocate a number of hours to each school and act as a crucial link between parents and school. They are normally employed to work with pupils/families with attendance problems and/or pupils at risk of exclusion. It is important to be aware of how to contact your ESW.

The pupil and his/her parents should be consulted and agree the targets. Communication of IEP targets to the whole-school staff, including Learning Support Assistants and supply teachers, is essential as consistency is the main therapeutic tool.

Targets

Through incident recording and teachers' observations, the school will be aware of the frequency and severity of behaviours. Specific difficulties should be identified and achievable targets set, with no more than three targets at any one time. It has been our experience that attending to specific behaviours clearly, directly and with adequate resources often indirectly clears up parallel behaviours. The EBD pupil does enjoy achieving and all the consequences of getting it right.

Targets need to be SMART, i.e. Specific, Manageable, Achievable, Realistic and Timed. For example:

◆ Peter should agree to sit happily where he is placed in class.

◆ Jack should contribute to class discussion only when asked.

◆ If Amy wishes to leave the classroom, she should do so only after pleasantly requesting permission. She should go straight to Miss Jones's room.

◆ If Ahmed wants attention he should use a quiet hand.

◆ Melissa will eat her lunch quietly with Mrs Roberts.

◆ John will attend the homework club on Tuesday and Thursday with Mr Brown to complete all homework.

◆ Alex will work in the blue room with Miss James for the last three periods of every day, quietly, with good manners and appropriate concentration.

◆ The school would like Emily to sit quietly through breaktime with Mrs Shaw.

Emotional and Behavioural Difficulties

Targets need to have time limits such as:

◆ by the end of the term

◆ for the two weeks starting . . . (set time interval)

◆ until the next meeting with parents.

In our experience EBD pupils know what to do and when they get it right. Remember they have a very accurate map of what is right and wrong.

In our EBD school we ran a daily points system regarding behaviour. When the pupils were asked to grade their own behaviour from 0 to 3 they almost always concurred with the teacher.

The IEP is a very significant tool for the management of pupils with EBD. It clearly draws a base line, saying 'This is where we are now'. A term later it is possible to evaluate progress and draw up new targets. It shows the pupil, parents and teacher how behaviour and learning have improved and what tactics work. It creates a climate of encouragement and hope.

School Action can be successful and the child can return to the wider field of 'regular' pupils. However, if behaviours continue to substantially and regularly inter-fere with the pupil's own learning or that of the class group, then following the IEP review, the school, in consultation with the parents, may decide to move to School Action Plus.

School Action Plus
At this stage the school seeks the advice of external professional services. In the case of a pupil with EBD this could mean a behaviour specialist, the educational

psychologist, a clinical psychologist, a social worker, a psychiatrist, the police, and ESW. If there are concerns regarding child abuse or a history of physical or neurological problems then other specialists may be involved (this could include a Child Protection Co-ordinator). The IEP is modified and meetings regarding the pupil's progress are held at least once a term and are attended by the relevant external specialists.

If, after reviewing the pupil's progress over a set period of time, there seems to be no progress, or a deterioration in the pupil's behaviour, the school may make a request to the LEA for a Statutory Assessment of the pupil. This assessment, managed by an LEA Officer, requests significant submissions from all involved with the pupil. Using this evidence the Officer decides if a Statement of Special Educational Needs should be written. This is a legal document and guarantees the provision of resources for the pupil, almost always enabling him/her to maintain his/her place in mainstream education. When requesting a Statutory Assessment the school has to supply information about interventions and their outcomes over time. This information will be contained in the IEPs.

Following the completion of the Statement the LEA becomes responsible for holding an Annual Review on the pupil's progress. In some extreme cases a child may gain a place in a special school or unit through the naming of a facility in the Statement. However, this option is increasingly rare.

Other formal interventions
A 'Pastoral Support Programme' (PSP) should be automatically set up for a pupil who has had several

fixed-term exclusions or who is identified as being at risk of failure at school through disaffection. The PSP can often be a way of managing difficult behaviour in school without going into the legal complexities of School Action and Statementing and could be appropriate for older pupils who are experiencing problems.

The school could consider placing a pupil in a Learning Support Unit. However, such units need to be well run and managed by professionals who interface significantly with the mainstream school.

Summary

You are much more likely to be successful with pupils with EBD if you are supported by good, consistently applied whole-school systems.

Remember that standards of behaviour were found to be satisfactory in schools where:

♦ there was a wide range of formal and informal rewards

♦ sanctions were fair and understood by pupils

♦ the curriculum matched the needs of the pupils

♦ lessons were well prepared

♦ teachers were secure in their knowledge of the subject

♦ marking was constructive

♦ standards of achievement were either satisfactory or better

♦ there were good extra-curricular activities.

(DFE, 1990–92)

Get to know the school systems for rewards and sanctions, its behaviour expectations, how you record incidents of difficult behaviour, what you do in a crisis and the structures for pastoral support for pupils.

Make sure that your teaching room lives up to the whole-school expectations in terms of being smart, interesting and well organized.

Be clear about the school's SEN structure and your involvement with it. Make sure you know which pupils have IEPs/PSPs, what their targets are and what your role is. Know what practical help you will receive in your classroom and insist on the advice and support to which you are entitled. Above all, try not to be daunted by pupils with Emotional and Behavioural Difficulties.

Strong leadership and clear, whole-school systems which support good behaviour and learning, will give you a huge leg up in your ability to be successful. Try hard to involve your EBD pupils in the positive systems and you may even change your perception of what 'EBD' stands for – from 'Extremely Bloody Difficult, Every Bloody Day' to 'Everyone's Biggest Dream'. It does happen.

Virtually all the pupils who came to our school were either about to be, or had already been, excluded from mainstream education.

A considerable percentage of leavers (45 per cent in the most successful year) returned to mainstream schools and stayed there.

Schools *can* make a difference and when they do it benefits pupils, their families and society.

7

Communicating With Parents

Parents are the adults you will be talking to, phoning, writing to and inviting to reviews. Given the often disrupted family backgrounds of EBD pupils, you must not assume that the people who have parental responsibility are the birth parents. It is essential that you know which adults have legal responsibility for parenting the pupil.

In this chapter the word *parent* refers to all adults who have parental responsibility for the child. These adults could be the natural parents, step parents, grandparents, foster parents, the Local Authority and carers identified by the legal parents.

Widespread support for involving parents in their children's learning grows out of convincing evidence that positive family involvement has beneficial effects on children's academic achievement, social competence and school quality (Henderson and Berla, 1994). Today's schools know this to be the case, but how they ensure that effective, positive involvement of parents actually happens is the key to its success.

So often the school's only contact with these parents is a negative one: the ominous brown envelope; the nasty phone call home in which parents are asked to 'please keep John at home' or invited to 'try another school'. None of these things are particularly therapeutic.

This is not easy work and there are many factors operating in schools which push working with families lower down the pecking order. Teachers have inadequate time and are too stressed by the demands of the classroom to take on yet another task. Parents may be difficult to engage in a partnership and doing so is therefore very time consuming. Teachers may lack the skills needed to work with families. Communication with other professional bodies working with families may be difficult.

Let us remind ourselves of the complexities of this SEN identified in Chapter 1:

> The majority of these pupils are, in reality, very unhappy, hovering as they do on the fringes of society. They are disabled from functioning normally by a complex interaction of causes ranging from genetic factors, through family difficulties including being exposed to physical and/or sexual abuse, to the pressures of a changing society. They are emotionally volatile and lack those qualities of stability and robustness which enable other pupils to survive similar pressures intact.

Research clearly shows that:

> A background of unemployment, poverty, crime, violence, abuse, alcohol, drugs, mental health and family break up, all feature largely in the statistics of young people who experience serious difficulties in school. (Scottish Executive, 2004: section 2.10)

The parents of these children very often live stressful lives. They may:

81

- ◆ have children who, through an inherited disability, are testing their parenting skills to the limit

- ◆ themselves be experiencing problems which are a causal factor in their child's SEN

- ◆ be a relative who is accommodating the child on an agreed Residence Order

- ◆ be fostering a very challenging child who has experienced significant abuse

- ◆ be working in the emotionally charged environment of a children's home.

It is our experience that working effectively with the parents of pupils with EBD is one of a school's most therapeutic tools but also one of the most challenging. In teaching pupils with this complex SEN one encounters the extremes of society. We have worked with devoted parents who have been appreciative, supportive and respectful and whose children have made tremendous progress. But we have also experienced, from parents, serious verbal and physical abuse, dishonesty, collusion with the pupil, drug and alcohol abuse, chaos, extreme neglect of their child and total despair.

Given the complexity of this SEN, the parents of EBD pupils will need very particular help. This can be most effectively done through giving them:

- ◆ clear policies and procedures

- ◆ good communication

- ◆ understanding, support and respect

- ◆ quick responses to problems and difficulties.

The LEA must be supporting you in your work with parents/carers through their SEN policy. They must make arrangements for parent-partnership services and ESW input and inform parents and schools about the arrangements for the services and how they can access them. Your head teacher has responsibility for SEN provision and should work closely with the school's SENCO and keep governors fully informed. Your governors determine, in co-operation with the head teacher, the school's general policy and approach to SEN, including descriptions of the systems you have in place for consulting with parents. They report to parents on the implementation of this policy and ensure that parents are notified of a decision by the school that SEN provision is being made for their child. Parents legally need to ensure that that their child receives an education either by regular attendance at school or otherwise. Educational Social Workers work with parents who are struggling to get their child to school.

The Code of Practice (DfES, 2001) describes parents as partners who should be empowered to:

◆ recognize and fulfil their responsibilities as parents and play an active and valued role in their child's education

◆ have knowledge of their child's entitlement within the SEN framework

◆ make their views known about how their child is educated

◆ have access to information, advice and support during assessment and any related decision-making processes about special educational provision.

Emotional and Behavioural Difficulties

As well as the school's SEN Policy there are three other school policies which are particularly pertinent for parents of pupils with EBD:

1. The whole-school Behaviour Policy – ensures a consistency of behaviour expectations across the school, understood and owned by all.

2. Policy on the use of physical force – identified in the pupils' IEP and supported by the school's and LEA's policy on physical interventions. Because EBD pupils can be volatile and may, on rare occasions, present significant physical management challenges, it is essential that the procedures for handling any physical threat that they may present to person or property are clearly described in their IEP and understood and agreed by parents (DfEE, 1998).

3. Child Protection Policy – your school's Child Protection Policy document must be clear and current and all staff must be familiar with its contents. Pupils with EBD are the most likely of all your school population to have experienced or are experiencing emotional, physical or sexual abuse. You need to be very clear about the presenting signals and the referral procedures. Your designated member of staff for child protection will give you support and guidance in this crucial but extremely delicate area.

Parents may not have read these policies, but they should be aware of their existence. Their importance is to state clearly that the school's systems have been set up to make it a safe and happy place for all its pupils.

Parents of pupils at our special school were made aware, on admission, that if physical management was necessary, there was a procedure that would be followed if the pupil, other members of the school, or school property were threatened. Parents were asked to sign this agreement. The majority willingly did so as they understood the importance of the policy in helping to keep their child safe.

Good communication

Try as hard as possible to make positive contact with parents. This will be time consuming and schools need to recognize the value of this work by allocating staff time.

♦ Writing positive letters home, making positive phone calls just for an informal chat, writing encouraging comments in a pupil's school diary and giving tangible rewards for a child's good behaviour all help to communicate to parents that you care for their child.

♦ Giving parents regular opportunities to discuss their child both informally and formally will help them to feel welcome in school. Agree the times with them and don't let them dominate unreasonably.

♦ Wherever possible pupils should be involved in all meetings with parents. However, there are times when just the managing adults should talk together. These separate meetings could be concerned with private matters which it might not be helpful for a pupil to know about, for example a parent's illness, a teacher's personal plans for the future, significant imminent changes which may destabilize the pupil.

♦ Making sure that parents understand school policies and procedures, are aware of how to access support in preparing their contributions to reviews, and are given documents to be discussed well in advance will enable them to feel involved in their child's education.

♦ Listen to parents' desires and aspirations regarding their child and assure them that the school will, wherever possible, fulfil their wishes.

Understanding, support and respect

The parents of children with EBD all have two things in common. First of all they are parents and, secondly, their child is being very challenging in school and probably at home as well. However, when forming a partnership with these parents you will meet people with greatly contrasting qualities and life experiences. Dislike of school, lack of confidence, great confidence, academic success, material success, inherited disabilities, poverty, divorce, illness, job stress, ethnic differences, language difficulties will all be encountered.

The following principles will help you to be effective:

♦ Make early contact with all parents, especially if their child is being difficult. Try to be flexible (as far as possible) about the time of a meeting.

♦ Warmly welcome the parents into school. Hold the meeting in a calm, pleasant place. Be on time and look smart. Hide your inclination to rush, rush, rush and present yourself as giving them all your attention and support. Don't sit behind a desk.

♦ Every parent is unique, will have different needs and will require different approaches. This may be stating the obvious; however, as we have explained, these particular parents are likely to be experiencing a greater degree of stress than normal so an individual approach is essential to a successful partnership. You may not know anything about the parents so your antennae, at the first meeting, will need to be very finely tuned. Are they hostile? What is their language ability? Are they educated, assertive, submissive, truthful, deceiving, disabled? These early observations will inform how you differentiate your approach.

♦ If you pick up signs of significant stress in the parent, acknowledge this with them and keep very calm. Never be judgemental. Alternatively, it might be appropriate to ignore their stress and act as normal. This might serve to calm things down. 'Thank you for coming', 'did you have a good journey here?', 'isn't it a lovely day?', etc. If the stress prevents the meeting from progressing, say things like 'you seem upset today, is everything alright?', 'Would you like a cup of tea?', 'I expect you're worried about Tim, but you know we're here to help him'. Keep calm and talk with care and assurance. If they respond with a confidence give positive acceptance and support. 'Thank you for telling me that, no wonder you're upset' (validating their feelings). 'Are you able to carry on with this meeting? We really do want to support you and Tim.'

Emotional and Behavioural Difficulties

♦ Always keep any data about the pupil available to read to the parent in a calm and objective way. Make sure the pupil's use of 'Anglo Saxon' is honestly related.

♦ Acknowledge and draw on the parents' knowledge and expertise in relation to their child. This will help them to feel valued and give them confidence.

♦ Always start a meeting with supportive statements about the child: 'Alice is very sensitive isn't she', 'Hasn't Billy got a lovely sense of humour'.

♦ Questions such as 'how is she at home?', 'have you any concerns?', 'what does he do at the weekends?', 'how does she get on with her sisters/brothers?', 'are there things which wind him up at home?' will, if you listen carefully to the answers, give you lots of valuable information.

♦ If a parent expresses concerns, acknowledge them. Parent: 'I'm worried about Jacob because he doesn't have any friends.' Teacher: 'I understand how that would concern you. Does he talk about any children at school? I know he sometimes spends time with Ahmed.'

♦ Don't be condescending or judgemental. Be brief, clear and specific. Recognize the child's difficulties but never blame the parents for them.

♦ Have, as the focus of the meeting, the child and what you all want rather than what you don't want.

♦ Use 'I' and 'we' rather than 'you' when talking to parents. This takes the focus away from blaming the

parent. Instead of 'you don't help him with his homework' use 'I am concerned that Jack isn't doing his
homework. What can we do to make this better?'
Make the school's homework policy clear: 'We as a
school have written this to help your child's learning
so it would be great if we could come up with a plan
to help him', 'I am concerned that Jon keeps disturbing other pupils in class. What do you think we could
do about this? Does he do this at home? What do
you do?'

♦ Respect the validity of differing perspectives and
  seek constructive ways of reconciling different
  viewpoints. This is a very difficult one. In your work
  you will encounter parents with very different values
  and viewpoints from your own. The way in which
  you reconcile these differences will have a significant effect on the quality of your partnership.
  Criticism will evoke resentment, defensiveness,
  guilt, depression, so aim to remain positive and
  avoid criticism even if, in your heart, you strongly
  disapprove.

Jon's mum wouldn't let him walk to school on his
own as she thought he would be unsafe. This was
preventing him from maturing. We didn't say
'you're keeping him as a baby by taking him to
school'. We found that 'He's so lucky to have such a
caring mum. Do you think he could manage the
walk? How would it help him? How could we help
you not to be so worried about it?' proved to be a
much more therapeutic way of approaching the
problem.

You will encounter parents whose problems are so severe that warm, positive, child-focused support will not begin to tackle the problem. Persist for a while but not for too long. For the sake of the pupil you will need to acquire inter-agency help.

♦ If there are child protection issues your ESW should be involved, as should Social Services. Local Authorities will have clear guidelines regarding all Child Protection procedures which you must follow. The police may need to be informed if the pupil is offending or has been sexually or physically abused. The pupil's GP should also be involved if there are concerns about physical or mental health as a consequence of abuse. For this multi-professional work, particularly, you will need to have very good documentary evidence to justify your concerns. 'He's very naughty a lot of the time' just won't do.

♦ You will also need excellent organizational skills or a great secretary.

Summary

Working in partnership with the parents of children with EBD can be challenging to say the least. However, if schools get it right the rewards in terms of the adjustment of the child can be very heartening.

This is often emotionally draining and time consuming work, and if the school does not recognize the energy, time and effort involved, and appreciate staff accordingly, it is unlikely to be successful.

EBD pupils and their parents need schools which:

♦ are well organized

♦ have clear policies understood and owned by all

♦ have good systems of communication with parents so that they are involved in their child's learning

♦ warmly welcome all parents into school.

Some parents will not engage and will need more intensive multi-disciplinary input. However, if a school strives to treat all parents with understanding, support and respect then they are giving their pupils with EBD the best possible chance.

8

Managing Major Challenges

Pupils identified as having EBD may be volatile and can occasionally present teachers with significantly challenging behaviour. This chapter will give teachers practical advice on how to manage these sometimes very alarming situations. It will suggest ways of anticipating difficulties, avoiding escalation, dealing with unstable pupils and deflecting potentially harmful situations.

The Elton Report (DES, 1989) stated that 1 per cent of teachers perceived behaviour in their school to be 'very serious' and 16 per cent perceived behaviour as 'serious'. Between 1 per cent and 2 per cent of teachers stated that they experienced physical abuse.

The document *Prevalence of Disability Among Children* (Bone and Meltzer, 1989) gives a figure of 2 per cent of the school population having profound EBD. This small but significant percentage of pupils can, if not correctly managed, dominate classes and in some cases parts of the school. They can attract peripheral, disconnected and disaffected pupils into an anti-school/adult/teacher/rules sub-culture, forming a hard core of difficult to manage pupils. This sub-group of pupils are more likely to be physically/verbally abusive to adults.

We need to accept that we are going to be faced, hopefully on rare occasions, with abusive behaviour from pupils. How we manage these serious incidents should be part of the whole school's policy for SEN.

Before you start teaching it is essential that you are aware of the systems of support available to you in the school.

Questions to ask:

♦ Can you give a red card to a pupil who has to leave your room immediately? What happens if he/she doesn't comply?

♦ Is there a fire brigade you can call on and is it reliable? The school should have a well-organized/ administered, smart response system that is available as soon as a teacher requires support. The speed at which a team responds can be crucial to the outcome and, consequently, to the possibility of threatening behaviours recurring.

♦ Is there a 'time out' place to which a pupil can be sent and is it always manned by experienced staff?

♦ Do any pupils you teach have an IEP with a handling policy attached to it, which gives direction for managing abusive, challenging behaviour?

♦ Are parents invited into school to help deal with difficult situations? Are class teachers involved?

♦ Does the school require all incidents to be recorded in writing? Is there a pro forma to complete and is it graded to denote seriousness?

The EBD pupils who are likely to present an abusive challenge to you are almost always the ones who create ongoing minor behaviour problems. They tend not to settle easily to work, have difficulties with routines and have significant relationship problems with other pupils in the group. They tend to have a high self-image and a low academic self-image and the tension between the two images can be the cauldron in which their anger is heated. They may have several triggers for their anger. It is these triggers that set them on the road to behaviours which become increasingly difficult to manage.

Here is a four-stage model for managing extreme behaviour. It should enable you to be more objective, calm and analytical when faced with significant abuse.

Stage 1: Initial trigger phase

Triggers normally start the escalation. We have all experienced them from being very tiny: 'Fat face', 'big nose', 'spotty', 'where do you get your clothes from, jumble sales?'

Regular pupils try to avoid triggers by looking away, ignoring the agitator and getting on with their work. For volatile EBD pupils, triggers can be the start of the escalation which ends with you taking the full heat. They look for triggers to wind themselves up, evident in comments such as 'stop him looking at me, he's winding me up'. A mainstream class is likely to contain children who mutually dislike each other, hate their best friend's mate, like aggravating those around them, etc. (just like the staffroom?). As a teacher you have to spot the dynamic, remove it, or simply stop it from happening.

Things to think about before the pupils come into the room include:

◆ How do you seat pupils in the classroom, separating groups, cliques, pairs and trios who generate difficulties?

◆ Do you seat some pupils next to your teaching base or change the seating arrangements to improve the atmosphere?

◆ How you announce test results needs to be carefully considered. Some delicate/sensitive pupils can find others knowing of their poor performance disturbing and humiliating.

◆ Whole-class testing can be difficult for pupils with poor performance skills and can cause considerable problems.

◆ Do you plan ahead to prevent disappointment? For example, if you know a trip has been cancelled tell the class well in advance, or don't announce a trip until it is certain to take place.

Here are a few triggers which occur every day. Some you can, to a degree, control; others are completely out of your control but can seriously affect the stability of the EBD pupil in your charge.

Emotional and Behavioural Difficulties

Trigger	Possible causes
Bad news	at home, mum/dad/relative/carer ill or had accident, friends ill/not in school, pet died
Criticism	poor academic scores, negative remarks (e.g. about clothes, hair, shoes, work, handwriting), accusation regarding negative behaviour (true or not)
Something bad is going to happen	going home to trouble, mum going into hospital, guilt following minor crime, drug taking, dad/step dad coming home
Something in school which causes anxiety is going to happen	homework, spelling test, exams, unfamiliar teacher, change of timetable, bullying, breaktime
Intimidation	from teacher, LSAs (some adults really think regular intimidation is a good tactic), another pupil, at home from dad/mum/brother/sister/ the lodger
Disappointment	poor test results, no football, lesson changes, unfulfilled promises
Expectations not fulfilled	poor performance, rejection by a girl/boy, different teacher
Irritation	aggravation from other children, name calling, noises, etc.

Remember, the regular pupil can normally tolerate poor organization, disappointment, incompetence, changes to lessons, failed trips, even a bit of intimidation, but our EBDs can be fragile, sensitive and egocentric. Everything that goes wrong is personal. Something as minor as a cancelled trip, postponed football match, or one small ill-advised remark can start a fire of resentment. With some classes it's all plainly there waiting to happen.

Tactics for removing triggers

This is a delicate process proving the old adage that 'It ain't what you do, it's the way that you do it'. Mistakes made here can escalate difficult behaviour rather than prevent it.

♦ Distract the disturbed pupil by setting a different task.

♦ Distract a small group by setting individuals within the group separate tasks which require their movement away from the hot spot.

♦ Speak quietly to the pupil who is causing the distraction, maintaining a calm expression and body posture.

♦ Don't always expect immediate obedience. Try to avoid 'eyeballing', however tempting it might be to confront the pupil head on. Allow the pupil to settle, giving them 'take-up time' to accept your request.

♦ Move your teaching position next to the distressed or difficult pupil.

♦ Pointedly ignore some behaviour. No reaction from you means no result!

♦ Engage the disturbed pupil with work or non-work-related conversation such as football, soap operas, TV, clothes, hair cuts and, once the pupil has quietened down, encourage him/her to return to the work set.

◆ Separate pupils as soon as the trouble starts. Often these challenging pupils find it difficult to change tack once they have set sail for the margin.

◆ If the lesson starts to get difficult, alter the lesson plan, alter the style and try to use a more exciting or calming method of delivery than earlier in the lesson. If you cannot remove the trigger then the pupil will constantly be angered by it. Some difficult pupils enjoy seeing the distress of others and will continue to make remarks and noises while denying all knowledge of their involvement. In fact, if pushed, they will themselves become the problem. You must NEVER become involved in such inter-changes as:

Teacher: 'Stop that.'
Pupil: 'What?'
Teacher: 'That noise you were making.'
Pupil: 'What noise? I wasn't making a noise.'
Teacher: 'I saw you making it.'
Pupil: 'Oh, you saw me making a noise, that's clever.'
(Class have a laugh)
Teacher: 'Stop making that noise. You're upsetting David.'
Pupil: 'No I was not.'
Teacher: 'Yes you were.'
Pupil: 'No I was not.'
Teacher: 'Yes you were.'
Pupil: 'I was not. What are you going to do about it?'

(Class wait with bated breath for teacher's reply)

This can destabilize the adult and pupils involved, creating tension and stress for the whole class. It is important for you NOT to be wound up in the heat of the situation, but to stay objective, calm and purposeful:

Teacher: 'I can hear a noise . . . (*pause*) . . . there it goes again.'

Teacher: 'Let's all be quiet and Brian can make the noise again.'

Pupil: 'I didn't make a noise.'

Teacher: 'Great, but in future if you feel you want to make a noise let us all know and we can listen.'

Pupil: 'Do you think that's clever?'

Teacher: 'Brian, we all know you are here, we like you and we are pleased to have you in class.'

Pupil: 'Why are you picking on me?'

Teacher: 'Sorry if you think that, Brian, but it's not true' . . . (*pause*) . . . We just want to work quietly.'

Teacher: 'Would you like me to help you, Brian?'

♦ On a very few occasions pupils will come to the classroom in turmoil as a result of unresolved complications in their lives. These could relate to goings-on inside or outside the family, events beyond their control, chemical imbalances and so on. Your classroom, other pupils and you as teacher are not responsible for the disturbance. These pupils are likely to 'erupt' at any time. You must know the school procedures for such an event and the names of the pupils who might behave in this way. The planned intervention should give the pupil time and space to talk through difficulties with a trusted adult.

Stage 2: Escalation

If angry pupils are not protected from humiliation or abuse by other pupils, or have triggers unresolved, then their negative behaviours are likely to escalate. Escalation normally takes the form of increased frequency of the behaviour stimulated by the triggers. Sometimes the pupil will develop a more personal, more specific behaviour just for you. The behaviour may be so significant that you are forced to respond. These can include:

Most difficult behaviour	plus	plus
Out of seat →	hindering other pupils →	threatening other pupils
Banging on the desk and/or making noises →	shouting out →	chanting
Rudeness →	talking out of turn →	refusing to answer questions
Throwing small objects →	pushing furniture around →	minor damaging of equipment/ furniture/self

If you do not swiftly intervene, the challenging behaviour is negatively reinforced and the spiral can very quickly escalate into violence. In these situations delayed gratification does not work. The disturbed individual needs some recognition of his/her distress NOW.

A teacher has the responsibility of protecting but not colluding with the distressed pupil. You should recognize the pupil's distress but not become partisan in his/her favour, or damning and judgemental. You should remain analytical, calm and above all objective, listening carefully and honestly to the anger and/or abuse.

Tactics for managing escalation

There are many dos and don'ts in these situations but be aware that whatever you do, including nothing, is crucial. When the atmosphere in the classroom is heated the class will be looking to you to calm it down. You have to think clearly and objectively about safely defusing the 'bomb' that is being constructed.

♦ You should talk slowly and in a controlled manner. Think about every word you use, choose phrases carefully and don't stutter.

♦ Direct eye contact may not be a good idea at this stage as it is too confrontational; the pupil may be agitated by it.

♦ Avoid all the classic win or lose statements like 'If you do that again . . .!'

♦ Make no threats as they simply give negative targets for the pupil to aim for. Repeat reasonable requests calmly but with a touch of insistence. You must sound confident.

> 'Would you sit down please?'
> 'Please sit down.'
> 'Would you sit down please?'
> 'Sit down please.'

Emotional and Behavioural Difficulties

♦ Try to carry on teaching closer to the problem and keep the rest of the class occupied. Ensure that the class is aware of what's happening. Make remarks such as 'I have a bit of a problem here. If you could all continue working quietly, it would be very helpful. Thank you.' Physical distance between you and the problem might send confused signals to the whole class: 'Is teacher frightened?', 'Can the teacher manage?' Too close, however, and a whole range of other problems come into play.

♦ Sometimes matching what the pupil says can be calming:

Pupil: 'This work is crap.'
Teacher: 'This work is crap.' (*Try to match the tempo of the pupil*)
Pupil: 'This work stinks.'
Teacher: 'This work stinks?'
Pupil: 'Yes it stinks.'
Teacher: 'OK, let's change it for you.'
Pupil: 'What for?'
Teacher: 'Well, I have some other work you might like.'
Pupil: 'What's that then?'

We are in the business of negotiating not confronting.

♦ If you can remove the triggers do. Send the pupil who is creating the trigger off to see the head teacher with a note asking that he/she receives a long wait. Rearrange the seating, activity, lesson, etc. while this pupil is out of the room. You must, however, make it quite clear that you are noting in writing all the behaviour as and when it occurs. You will be surprised how writing down a behaviour as it happens can calm a situation.

A colleague of ours was once involved with a pupil who was acting out and using a great deal of expletives in the middle of a lesson. The teacher started to write it all down, quietly pronouncing each swear word as it was uttered. The pupil quickly recognized what the teacher was doing and said, 'What are you doing that for?' The teacher replied, 'Well, when I see your parents, maybe tonight, I want to make sure I have written every single word you have used towards me and some members of the class.' 'Oh no, don't do that sir; my mother would kill me.' End of that particular problem. 'Sir' was used as a term of address from then on.

You can, of course, combine any of the tactics described above but please note three key points:

1. Ensure that no sudden changes of attitude or expectation are made.

2. Stay calm and don't make any quick movements.

3. Be clear and consistent.

Stage 3: Negative choice and crisis stage

You will be aware that the pathways to extremely difficult behaviour are idiosyncratic and often relate to the individual pupil's feelings of vulnerability. Some pupils will become angry very quickly; others may be a little angry all the time. Some pupils will have a violent outburst about what appears to be very little; others 'blow up' rarely but when they do it's extremely difficult to manage them. Most abusive behaviours towards an adult normally occur when the adult tries to correct a behaviour or prevent a dangerous situation arising.

Very angry pupils have physiological symptoms which are worth keeping in mind:

♦ the brain tells the body to get ready for action

♦ blood pressure increases

♦ teeth become clenched

♦ shoulders rise

♦ the production of red corpuscles speeds up

♦ the heart pumps faster

♦ digestive secretions stop

♦ fists become tight, palms sweaty

♦ the rectum and bladder become harder to empty

♦ feet can become twitchy.

The pupil is building up to fight or flee and you might also be developing the same symptoms. This is a situation which has to be managed with great care and objectivity otherwise you can be swept into the maelstrom. You have to be aware of how you are feeling but must appear calm and on top of the situation.

Get your breathing as near to normal as possible. Sweating and panting do not express calmness. Try not to clench your fists but leave them open, palms facing towards the angry pupil, giving the impression of appeasement. Try to stand still. Keep your shoulders relaxed and whatever you do don't clench your teeth.

When assessing the risk of violence you should consider the following:

1. Is the pupil I am dealing with facing a high level of stress?

2. Does the pupil have a handling policy? If so, what is it?

3. Does the pupil have a history of very challenging behaviour?

4. Has the pupil verbally abused me or another member of staff in the past?

5. Has the pupil threatened me or another member of staff with violence in the past?

6. Has the pupil attacked adults in the school before?

At Stage 3 the pupil is almost out of control of his/her own feelings and behaviour. He/she may say outlandish things to provoke you or another member of the class. A level of frustration has set in which the pupil cannot resolve and the previous behaviour now becomes more invasive and potentially more dangerous.

The pupil starts to interact dangerously in a way that requires interventions of a significant type.

Behaviour	Secondary	Consequence
Starting to shout out at another pupil	→ threatening pupil in voice and posture	→ other pupil responds, fight ensues
Ripping up textbook	→ throwing things about	→ throwing things at other pupils
Pushing furniture	→ turning furniture over	→ pushing bigger and bigger things around

Tactics for managing the crisis stage

You must summon support at this stage. There should be procedures in place in the school which provide immediate help. Until that help arrives it is important that the behaviour is contained and that pupils are not hurt and property damaged, either of which could escalate the behaviour further.

♦ Maintain good, strong eye contact with the troubled pupil and any other pupil/pupils involved.

♦ Keep your mouth moist, talk slowly and clearly.

♦ Maintain good body posture, straight back, relaxed shoulders.

♦ Do not mention punishment/sanctions at this crisis time. Threatening detention etc. is simply setting negative behaviour targets. No physical prompting should be attempted unless training has been given and you are happy to use such techniques.

♦ Persuade the pupil to move to a quiet place. Keep talking in a strong and calm way, referring to the fact that support has been sent for and how being quieter now would be really helpful. Listen for any change of tone or content which can be reflected back, such as:

Pupil: 'Don't come near me, OK. Stay away.'
Teacher: 'OK.'
Pupil: 'Stay away.'
Teacher: 'OK.'
Pupil: 'You can shove your work up your a***!'
Teacher: 'Hey, I worked hard to produce the work, that's rude.'
Pupil: 'Yeah, but the work's crap.'
Teacher: 'OK, but that's rude.'
Pupil: 'Yeah, but the work's crap.'
Teacher: 'You don't have to be rude. I prepared that work for you.' (*With a less strong voice*)
Pupil: 'Yeah.'
Teacher: 'I come to work every day, because I like teaching you.'
Pupil: 'You're mad.'
Teacher: 'I like mad; it's better than swearing.'

We are beginning to ease the tension and calm the situation down.

♦ Make sure the pupil is aware that there are clear pathways to the door and you have no intention of preventing him/her from leaving. However, it should be expressed that leaving the classroom would not help the situation and calm settled behaviour is the target.

♦ Another tactic might be to ask the pupil to stay and ask the class to leave quietly.

♦ To prevent the pupil becoming too powerful by monopolizing all of your attention, try to keep teaching the whole class by pointing to the work set and referring to the learning targets, allowing the delivery of the curriculum to be interrupted as little as possible. Speak honestly to them: 'Thanks for being supportive, it really helps. Please continue with your work.'

Stage 4: Recovery phase

When the behaviour seems to be mellowing and the pupil is calming down your work is not yet finished. At this stage the pupil is still vulnerable and can become angry again quite quickly if not properly managed. Congratulate the pupil for calming down. Be visibly impressed by good manners and adequate conversation, but don't over do the positive. Find a quiet safe place for him/her to sit away from the class and pupil/pupils who may aggravate the situation again. Even without external stimulation the pupil could still erupt as some internal feelings might still be sore. Watch out for raised voices, any anxiety in conversation or return to flight/fight symptoms.

Talk through what has happened quietly; trying to recover the previous calmer relationship. Make allowances for guilt feelings and a need for some pupils to apologize almost continually. This recovery work should preferably be done by the class teacher while the relief staff member continues the whole-class teaching, or by support staff who should have training in this sort of counselling.

If damage has been done to the classroom, furniture,

equipment or books, be supportive about putting those things back together. This should be undertaken as quickly as possible after the event; putting chairs upright, straightening furniture, repairing equipment and perhaps using tape to put objects like textbooks back together.

If professional repairs are needed, involve the pupil in ordering materials and ringing up the services responsible for fixing the items. Make a long-term plan with the pupil to improve the environment in which the incident occurred and wherever possible involve the pupil in supporting the craftsmen who make the repairs.

If other adults have been involved in the incident of abuse make sure the pupil is able to meet them and chat through what happened. The pupil cannot be coerced or forced into making an apology as that may reawaken the pain. However, if Stage 4 is carefully managed it would be unusual for an apology not to be forthcoming.

If other pupils are involved, then the reintroduction of the recovered pupil has to be well managed. Unless it is a new class, the teacher should have a clear picture of the relationships within the group and understand some of the dynamics which hold together and blow apart the different clusters and cliques within it. If there has been a major confrontation between two pupils this has to be resolved before the class can continue.

A colleague once witnessed a dreadful fight at breaktime which he had to physically stop and staff had to settle the two boys down afterwards in separate rooms. They were finally brought back together outside the classroom and the incident was talked through. As the pupils were now calm the teacher brought them back into the classroom and sat them at the front on the same double desk! After a short while they started to argue again. Instead of moving the boys apart, the teacher went through the incident and previous conversations, sitting them back at the double desk but now having to share the same chair! This teacher was saying clearly 'we've done the fighting, the talking, the quietening, now it's time for you to do the work'. This was a strong, confident and intelligent teacher.

If there are a group of pupils involved who provoked or maybe caused the abusive behaviour, they should be encouraged to think through the incident chronologically. Led by the teacher they must accept some responsibility and consequently some modification of their behaviours before the recovered pupil can be reintroduced.

Throughout Stage 4 you should try to maintain a sense of optimism and lead positively throughout.

> The more positive the outcome the less likely the behaviour is to recur.

Summary

Human behaviour is never easy to predict, but a clear structure of responses to complex and threatening behaviour is essential. Placing behaviours in a framework of four stages can help you to understand what is happening and develop strategies which can prevent the more extreme behaviours from occurring. This ensures that you remain calm and objective when confronted with a serious behaviour. If you are observant, understand the significance of triggers for EBD pupils, and recognize the signs of escalation, you will be less likely to make basic mistakes which can in themselves actually cause escalation.

On occasions, however, and despite your best efforts, the pupil will 'erupt'. The school systems in place for supporting teachers and pupils at this crisis point, the methods employed for reparation and follow-up support for the teacher and the pupil will have a significant effect on the likelihood of the behaviour recurring.

Conclusion

In this book we have described carefully selected, key interventions aimed at supporting your work with pupils with Emotional and Behavioural Difficulties. You are going to meet these pupils in mainstream schools and some will succeed in putting you off balance, making you doubt your ability and competence. We have learnt over many years of teaching that there are ways of working with these pupils which will allow you to recover your sense of balance and move forward creatively. Don't be hard on yourself when things are difficult – think clearly, objectively, dip into our book and find a way to resolve the problem. It *is* possible to enjoy the challenge and teach with optimism when faced with this difficult and bewildering SEN. We've been there.

EBD pupils demand more of you and your school than any other SEN and often give the least back in return. However, we have followed many classes and individual pupils round schools, observing them being managed by different teachers. We know that teachers do make a difference, classes do settle, and difficult pupils do stop being challenging when the school and the teacher get it right.

References

Bone, M. and Meltzer, H. (1989), *The Prevalence of Disability Among Children*, OPCS Survey. London: HMSO.

Cole, T., Visser, J. and Upton, G. (1998), *Effective Schooling for Pupils with Emotional and Behavioural Difficulties*. London: David Fulton Publishers.

Darwin, C. (1999), *The Expression of the Emotions in Man and Animals* [1872], ed. P. Eckman. London: Fontana Press.

DES (1989), *Discipline in Schools: Report of the Committee of Enquiry Chaired by Lord Elton*. London: HMSO.

DFE (1990–92), *Education for Disaffected Pupils*. London: Ofsted.

DFE (1994), *Pupils with Problems*, Circular 9/94. London: DFE.

DfEE (1998), *Section 550A of the Education Act 1996: The Use of Force to Control or Restrain Pupils*. London: DfEE.

DfES (2001), *Special Educational Needs Code of Practice*. London: DfES.

Emler, N. (2001), *Self-esteem: The Costs and Causes of Low Self-worth*. London: Joseph Rowntree Foundation/York Publishing Services.

Hargreaves, D. (1967), *Social Relations in a Secondary School*. London: Routledge.

Henderson, A. and Berla, N. (1994), *A New Generation of Evidence: The Family is Critical to Student Achievement*. Colombia, MD: National Committee for Citizens in Education.

Mortimore, P. (1987), *ILEA Junior School Project*. London: ILEA.

Rutter, M., Maughan, B., Mortimore, P. and Ouston, J. (1979), *Fifteen Thousand Hours: Secondary Schools and Their Effects on Children*. Cambridge, MA: Harvard University Press.

Rutter, M. and Smith, D. J. (eds) (1995), *Psychosocial Disorders in Young People: Time Trends and Their Causes*. Chichester: Wiley.

Scottish Executive (2004), *Better Behaviour–Better Learning. Report of the Discipline Task Group*. London: HMSO.

Underwood, J. E. A. (1955), *Report of the Committee on Maladjusted Children*. London: HMSO.

Webster-Stratton, C. (1999), *How to Promote Children's Social and Emotional Competence*. London: Paul Chapman Publishing.

Winnicott, D. M. (1964), *The Child, the Family and the Outside World*. London: Penguin.